What
Shall
^{the}Redeemed
Wear?

What Shall the Redeemed Wear?

with Study Questions.

Simon Schrock

Vision Publishers, Inc.
Harrisonburg, VA

First Printing 2000
Second Printing 2005

What Shall the Redeemed Wear?
ISBN: 1-932676-07-4

Unless otherwise noted all Scripture references are
from the King James Version of the Holy Bible.

Published by Vision Publishers, Inc.
Harrisonburg, Virginia

Layout Artist: Craig Wenger
Cover Design: Lonnie Yoder

For additional copies or comments write to:
Vision Publishers, Inc.
P.O. Box 190
Harrisonburg, VA 22803
Phone (877) 488-0901
Fax (540) 437-1969
E-mail: visionpubl@ntelos.net
(see order form in back)

Table of Contents

with Study Questions

Preface

"You're not going to wear that, are you?" Such questions often lead into quarrelsome conflicts. Dad asks his son to wear pants that look more decent, and Mom is not happy with her daughter's selection of clothing. As parents well know, there is a conflict between the younger and older on what to wear.

One way to stir up strife in the church is to register a concern about immodesty and following the latest ridiculous fad in so-called dress. The conflict is fueled by those who say God doesn't care how you dress. They reinforce it by claiming that God looks on the heart, not the outward appearance.

Is that really what the Bible says? Is it true that God doesn't care how His children dress themselves? That is not what I found as I studied the Scriptures on this subject.

Is this only a parent-teenager, older-versus-younger conflict? It is bigger than that. The conflict began after Adam and Eve yielded to Satan in the garden of Eden. It is a spiritual battle in which Satan and the world have declared war on Christ and the church.

Since clothing is a statement of who we are, I write from a concern that those who confess the name of

Jesus will honor Him in all things, including the clothing they wear.

I write this from the battlefield, not the victory pageant. While I enjoy being free from the world of fashion, I continue to be in the battle to challenge God's people to experience the joy of being set free from addiction to the latest fad and fashion. That is the reason for this book, "What Shall the Redeemed Wear?"

> "I will greatly rejoice in the LORD, my soul shall be joyful in my God; for he hath clothed me with the garments of salvation, he hath covered me with the robe of righteousness . . ." (Isaiah 61:10).

Simon Schrock
March 5, 2000

CHAPTER 1

Who Are the Redeemed?

A story is told about a pastor who met a boy in front of the church carrying a rusty bird cage. Inside the cage were two little birds fluttering around the bottom.

The pastor said, "Son, where did you get those birds?" The boy answered, "I trapped them out in the field." "What are you going to do with them?" the pastor asked. "I'm going to take them home and play with them and have some fun with them." Then the preacher asked, "What will you do with them when you get through playing with them?" "Oh," said the boy, "I guess I'll just feed them to an old cat we have around the house."

Then the preacher asked how much he would take for the birds. The boy answered, "Mister, you don't want these birds. They're just little old field birds and they can't sing very well."

The preacher replied, "I'll give you two dollars for the birds and the cage."

"All right," said the boy, "it's a deal, but you're making a bad bargain."

The exchange was made, and the boy went whistling down the street, happy because he had two dollars in his pocket. The preacher took the cage out behind the church and opened the door of the cage. The birds flew out and went soaring into the blue, singing as they went.

The next Sunday the preacher took the empty bird cage to the pulpit to use in illustrating his sermon. Then he said, "The little boy said the birds could not sing very well, but when I released them from the cage, they went singing away into the blue, and it seemed as though they were singing, *redeemed, redeemed, redeemed!*"[1]

The story of these birds is an illustration of redemption. The story of redemption in the Bible begins with two people who were caught and trapped in a cage of sin. Not only were they caught, but all of their offspring after them would be born inside this cage of sin. After Adam and Eve sinned against God, they were driven from their paradise of Eden into the world and the cage of sin. They once enjoyed the freedom and habitat of a perfect sinless environment. Now they are captured in a cage of sin. They lost their godly glory; they were naked and ashamed before God and had no song to sing.

The only hope of a song to sing was in a little spark of a promise from God before He drove them out of Eden. The hope of a song to sing was that the spark would burst into a bright light, "to give light to them that sit in darkness and in the shadow of death, to guide our feet into the way of peace" (Luke 1:79). "A light to lighten the Gentiles, and the glory of thy people

Israel" (Luke 2:32). Their hope was that this light would be a Redeemer, One who would come and open the door of the cage of sin and release them.

The message of redemption is woven throughout the Scriptures like a scarlet thread in an Amish quilt. It goes from one end to the other.

Insights from the Scriptures on redemption

The Bible refers to redeem, redeemer, redemption, etc., at least 160 times. What do the words mean as they are used in the Bible?

- to buy back
- to set someone free by paying a ransom
- to rescue from loss
- something to loosen with

Let us look at several Scriptures that speak of redemption.

Jacob was sick and near the end of life. Joseph and his sons came to visit him. When Grandpa Jacob learned that his grandsons were at his bedside, he said, "Bring them unto me, I want to bless them" (Genesis 48:9).

> "And he blessed Joseph, and said, God, before whom my fathers Abraham and Isaac did walk, the God which fed me all my life long unto this day, the Angel which redeemed me from all evil, bless the lads; and let my name be named on them, and the name of my fathers Abraham and Isaac; and let them grow into a multitude in the midst of the earth" (Genesis 48:15, 16).

In this blessing Jacob refers to the "angel which redeemed me from all evil." Here, *redeemed* describes rescuing, saving him from his troubles.

> "Then sang Moses and the children of Israel this song unto the LORD, and spake, saying, I will sing unto the LORD, for he hath triumphed gloriously: the horse and his rider hath he thrown into the sea" (Exodus 15:1).

Here were Moses and the Children of Israel singing a song of praise to the Lord for deliverance at the Red Sea.

> "Thou in thy mercy hast led forth the people which thou hast redeemed: thou hast guided them in thy strength unto thy holy habitation" (Exodus 15:13).

In this song Israel recognizes that God redeemed (rescued, saved) them from the Egyptian army.

> "But because the LORD loved you, and because he would keep the oath which he had sworn unto your fathers, hath the LORD brought you out with a mighty hand, and redeemed you out of the house of bondmen, from the hand of Pharaoh king of Egypt" (Deuteronomy 7:8).

Here is a reminder that God redeemed Israel out of the hand of Pharaoh, king of Egypt. God brought Israel out of the "cage" of slavery.

About the time David was anointed king he referred to God as "my strength and redeemer."

> "Let the words of my mouth, and the meditation of my heart, be acceptable in thy sight, O LORD, my strength, and my redeemer" (Psalm 19:14).

Jeremiah gave credit to the Lord for redeeming his life.

> "O Lord, thou hast pleaded the causes of my soul; thou hast redeemed my life" (Lamentations 3:58).

Here redemption is like a rescue. God rescued Jeremiah out of the judgment that was upon Israel.

Anna, an 84-year-old widow who worshiped God through fasting and prayer, stayed at the temple. She was at the temple when Jesus was brought there to present Him to the Lord.

Luke 2:38 tells us what she did.

> "And she coming in that instant gave thanks likewise unto the Lord, and spake of him to all them that looked for redemption in Jerusalem."

She talked about Jesus to those who were waiting for God to free—redeem—Israel. I can imagine she was telling the people that Jesus is the Redeemer of Israel. Jesus is the one who will free the people from the cage of sin . . . and give them a song.

Jesus did come to hang on the cross and become an open shame and curse to redeem you from sin.

> "Christ purchased our freedom (redeeming us) from the curse (doom) of the Law's (condemnation), by [Himself] becoming a curse for us, for it is written [in the Scriptures], Cursed is everyone who hangs on a tree (is crucified); [Deuteronomy 21:13] to the end that through [their receiving] Christ Jesus, the blessing [promised] to Abraham might come upon the Gentiles, so that we through faith might [all] receive [the realization of] the promise of the (Holy) Spirit" (Galatians 3:13, 14, Amplified).

Jesus paid the ransom price to deliver you from the cage and bondage of sin.

> "But when the fulness of the time was come, God sent forth his Son, made of a woman, made under the law, to redeem them that were under the law, that we might receive the adoption of sons" (Galatians 4:4, 5).

7

Jesus came to redeem them that are under the law. The price He paid was a sufficient ransom to release you from sin's prison.

Being redeemed means having forgiveness of sins.

"In whom we have redemption through his blood, the forgiveness of sins, according to the riches of his grace" (Ephesians 1:7).

It means we are His purchased possession.

"Which is the earnest of our inheritance until the redemption of the purchased possession, unto the praise of his glory" (Ephesians 1:14).

Redeemed here means setting free for a ransom—paying ransom for a criminal condemned to death. It releases me from the cage of sin and gives me a song to sing.

"Who hath delivered us from the power of darkness, and hath translated us into the kingdom of his dear Son: in whom we have redemption through his blood, even the forgiveness of sins" (Colossians 1:13, 14).

"Neither by the blood of goats and calves, but by his own blood he entered in once into the holy place, having obtained eternal redemption for us. For if the blood of bulls and of goats, and the ashes of an heifer sprinkling the unclean, sanctifieth to the purifying of the flesh: how much more shall the blood of Christ, who through the eternal Spirit offered himself without spot to God, purge your conscience from dead works to serve the living God? And for this cause he is the mediator of the new testament, that by means of death, for the redemption of the transgressions that were under the first testament, they which are called might receive the promise of eternal inheritance" (Hebrews 9:12-15).

Christ has secured a complete redemption with an everlasting release from sin's bondage.

"For they themselves shew of us what manner of entering in we had unto you, and how ye turned to God from idols to serve the living and true God; and to wait for his Son from heaven, whom he raised from the dead, even Jesus, which delivered us from the wrath to come" (1 Thessalonians 1:9, 10).

Christ delivers His children from the wrath to come. Hell was made for the devil and his angels and those who follow him. Christ came to redeem you from the wrath of God that will send the devil to hell.

Jesus Christ is the Redeemer.

He is the one who paid the ransom price to rescue you from the curse of sin . . . and gave you a song to sing!

He gives forgiveness of sin through the ransom price of His shed blood.

He is the one who gives the inheritance to His kingdom. He is the one who makes His purchased possession.

Who are the non-redeemed?

Before looking at who the redeemed are, let's first look at *who are the non-redeemed?*

"And he spake a parable unto them, saying, The ground of a certain rich man brought forth plentifully: and he thought within himself, saying, What shall I do, because I have no room where to bestow my fruits? And he said, This will I do: I will pull down my barns, and build greater; and there will I bestow all my fruits and my goods. And I will say to my soul, Soul, thou hast much goods laid up for many years; take thine ease, eat, drink, and be merry. But God said unto him, Thou fool, this night thy soul shall be required of thee: then whose shall those things be, which thou hast provided? So is he that

9

layeth up treasure for himself, and is not rich toward God" (Luke 12:16-21).

Possessions kept this man from God's provision of redemption.

> "Two men went up into the temple to pray; the one a Pharisee, and the other a publican. The Pharisee stood and prayed thus with himself, God, I thank thee, that I am not as other men are, extortioners, unjust, adulterers, or even as this publican. I fast twice in the week, I give tithes of all that I possess. And the publican, standing afar off, would not lift up so much as his eyes unto heaven, but smote upon his breast, saying, God be merciful to me a sinner. I tell you, this man went down to his house justified rather than the other: for every one that exalteth himself shall be abased; and he that humbleth himself shall be exalted" (Luke 18:10-14).

Self-righteousness hindered this man from seeing his need of redemption.

In brief, the unredeemed are those who seek earthly possessions rather than God's redemption. They are those good people who keep most of the laws, they go to church and do religious things. But they do not see themselves as caught in the trap of sin. Therefore they do not seek redemption.

They are those who are self-willed and self-sufficient, and will not yield their lives and possessions to Jesus Christ the Redeemer.

Where do the non-redeemed go after death?

> "There was a certain rich man, which was clothed in purple and fine linen, and fared sumptuously every day: and there was a certain beggar named Lazarus, which was laid at his gate, full of sores, and desiring to be fed

10

with the crumbs which fell from the rich man's table: moreover the dogs came and licked his sores. And it came to pass, that the beggar died, and was carried by the angels into Abraham's bosom: the rich man also died, and was buried; and in hell he lift up his eyes, being in torments, and seeth Abraham afar off, and Lazarus in his bosom. And he cried and said, Father Abraham, have mercy on me, and send Lazarus, that he may dip the tip of his finger in water, and cool my tongue; for I am tormented in this flame. But Abraham said, Son, remember that thou in thy lifetime receivedst thy good things, and likewise Lazarus evil things: but now he is comforted, and thou art tormented. And beside all this, between us and you there is a great gulf fixed: so that they which would pass from hence to you cannot; neither can they pass to us, that would come from thence" (Luke 16:19-26).

The rich man had no song to sing. He could not sing "redeemed!" He could cry in sorrow and pain.

"When the Son of man shall come in his glory, and all the holy angels with him, then shall he sit upon the throne of his glory: and before him shall be gathered all nations: and he shall separate them one from another, as a shepherd divideth his sheep from the goats: and he shall set the sheep on his right hand, but the goats on the left" (Matthew 25:31-33).

"Then shall he say also unto them on the left hand, Depart from me, ye cursed, into everlasting fire, prepared for the devil and his angels: . . . and these shall go away into everlasting punishment: but the righteous into life eternal" (Matthew 25:41, 46).

"And the devil that deceived them was cast into the lake of fire and brimstone, where the beast and the false prophet are, and shall be tormented day and night for ever and ever. And death and hell were cast into the lake of fire. This is the second death. And whosoever was not found written in the book of life was cast into the lake of fire" (Revelation 20:10, 14, 15).

When the noted agnostic Robert Ingersoll died, the printed funeral notice said, "There will be no singing."

Without God, without Christ, without redemption, what is there to sing about?

There is a message to the non-redeemed in Revelation, chapter three. This message is given to the Laodicean church. The people of this church were rich with the goods of this world. They had money and industry. The city was a prominent trading post, a center for banking and finance, and was noted for manufacturing fine glossy garments. It was famous for its school of medicine and eyesalve.

Notice God's message to them:

> "Because thou sayest, I am rich, and increased with goods, and have need of nothing; and knowest not that thou art wretched, and miserable, and poor, and blind, and naked: I counsel thee to buy of me gold tried in the fire, that thou mayest be rich; and white raiment, that thou mayest be clothed, and that the shame of thy nakedness do not appear; and anoint thine eyes with eyesalve, that thou mayest see" (Revelation 3:17, 18).

This was a city known for making garments. They probably wore the finest clothing money could buy. But God counsels them:

"You need the white robes of salvation."

"You stand spiritually naked before me."

"I, God, see the very core of evil in the center of your hearts."

> "Neither is there any creature that is not manifest in his sight: but all things are naked and opened unto the eyes of him with whom we have to do" (Hebrews 4:13).

As the non-redeemed stand before God, they do so in the shame of nakedness, the shame of their sins not being covered by the blood of the Redeemer.

They will not be clothed with the garment of salvation and praise or the robe of righteousness.

The unredeemed will be caught in the spiritual condition described by John in Revelation 16:15.

> "Behold, I come as a thief. Blessed is he that watcheth, and keepeth his garments, lest he walk naked, and they see his shame" (Revelation 16:15).

The unredeemed will stand before God in the shame of their sins and will hear this verdict:

"Depart from me, you workers of iniquity."

Who, then, are the redeemed?

> "And the publican, standing afar off, would not lift up so much as his eyes unto heaven, but smote upon his breast, saying, God be merciful to me a sinner. I tell you, this man went down to his house justified rather than the other: for every one that exalteth himself shall be abased; and he that humbleth himself shall be exalted" (Luke 18:13, 14).

This publican realized he was in the cage of sin. He realized he had a sinful heart. He realized he stood before a God who could see the very core of his heart. He came to God with a heart of repentance. He came with a humble and contrite spirit. He begged God for mercy and forgiveness. He went home justified.

The redeemed are those who realize and confess they are in the cage of sin. They are the ones who come to the Redeemer in repentance as they realize their condition before God. They are the ones who put their faith and trust in the ransom of blood Jesus Christ paid for them. They are the ones who with humble and contrite spirits ask to be forgiven. They are the ones who deny themselves and take up their cross and follow the Redeemer. Who are the redeemed?

"And he said, A certain man had two sons: and the younger of them said to his father, Father, give me the portion of goods that falleth to me. And he divided unto them his living. And not many days after the younger son gathered all together, and took his journey into a far country, and there wasted his substance with riotous living. And when he had spent all, there arose a mighty famine in that land; and he began to be in want. And he went and joined himself to a citizen of that country; and he sent him into his fields to feed swine. And he would fain have filled his belly with the husks that the swine did eat: and no man gave unto him. And when he came to himself, he said, How many hired servants of my father's have bread enough and to spare, and I perish with hunger! I will arise and go to my father, and will say unto him, Father, I have sinned against heaven, and before thee, and am no more worthy to be called thy son: make me as one of thy hired servants. And he arose, and came to his father. But when he was yet a great way off, his father saw him, and had compassion, and ran, and fell on his neck, and kissed him. And the son said unto him, Father, I have sinned against heaven, and in thy sight, and am no more worthy to be called thy son. But the father said to his servants, Bring forth the best robe, and put it on him; and put a ring on his hand, and shoes on his feet: and bring hither the fatted calf, and kill it; and let us eat, and be merry: for this my son was dead, and is alive again; he was lost, and is found. And they began to be merry" (Luke 15:11-24).

Notice the steps that bring him back into the arms of his father. He said:

"I am in one big mess in this 'hog cage.' Here I am eating with the pigs. If I were back with my father, I could live a clean life and have plenty of food to eat. I will repent. I will return to my father. I will tell him—'Dad, I'm a big sinner.' Maybe my father will take me back."

He puts his repentant heart into action. He left the pigpen behind and headed toward home and said, "Father, I have sinned!"

The father replied: "Son, the price is paid. You're forgiven! Here is the best robe possible for you. Wear this, and no one will see the scars of the pigpen. Put this robe on and come into my banquet hall. Let us celebrate! I want to tell my friends, 'This is my son, in a brand new robe! Let's have music!'"

The redeemed have garments of salvation.

> "I will greatly rejoice in the LORD, my soul shall be joyful in my God; *for he hath clothed me with the garments of salvation, he hath covered me with the robe of righteousness,* as a bridegroom decketh himself with ornaments, and as a bride adorneth herself with her jewels" (Isaiah 61:10).

The redeemed are clothed with the garment of salvation and a robe of righteousness. It is given to them by the Redeemer, Jesus Christ. In addition to a new robe they have new power.

- The Spirit that dwells in them will enable them to drive past the liquor store and not stop.
- They will have power to see a woman and not lust after her in a fantasy world.
- They will have power to say no to mundane activities and to gather for prayer and worship with other saints.

- They will have power to forgive others and be released from a bitter spirit.
- They will have power to cheerfully give to others in need.
- They will have power to witness of their hope in Christ their Redeemer.

Who are the redeemed? They are the ones with the garment of salvation. They walk in the robe of righteous living and their make-up is a song of redemption.

Where do the redeemed go after this life?

The Apostle John can give us some revelation on that subject.

> "Thou hast a few names even in Sardis which have not defiled their garments; and they shall walk with me in white: for they are worthy. He that overcometh, the same shall be clothed in white raiment; and I will not blot out his name out of the book of life, but I will confess his name before my Father, and before his angels. He that hath an ear, let him hear what the Spirit saith unto the churches" (Revelation 3:4-6).

Where will the redeemed go?

- They will be saints in God's presence.
- Their names will be in the book of life.
- They will be arrayed in the glory of white garments.
- Jesus will declare before the Father and the angels, "This is my redeemed child, who has put on the garment of salvation."

> "And they sung a new song, saying, Thou art worthy to take the book, and to open the seals thereof: for thou wast slain, and hast redeemed us to God by thy blood out of every kindred, and tongue, and people, and nation" (Revelation 5:9).

16

The redeemed will be singing a new song of praise to the Redeemer.

> "After this I beheld, and, lo, a great multitude, which no man could number, of all nations, and kindreds, and people, and tongues, stood before the throne, and before the Lamb, clothed with white robes, and palms in their hands" (Revelation 7:9).

Here the redeemed are in white robes, with palms in their hands. They are declaring and shouting, "Salvation to our God, which sitteth upon the throne, and unto the Lamb."

> "And I heard a voice from heaven, as the voice of many waters, and as the voice of a great thunder: and I heard the voice of harpers harping with their harps: and they sung as it were a new song before the throne, and before the four beasts, and the elders: and no man could learn that song but the hundred and forty and four thousand, which were redeemed from the earth. These are they which were not defiled with women; for they are virgins. These are they which follow the Lamb whithersoever he goeth. These were redeemed from among men, being the firstfruits unto God and to the Lamb" (Revelation 14:2-4).

The redeemed are the people with the garment of salvation, the robe of righteousness, and a new song of praise to their Redeemer.

The redeemed are the ones who will meet their Maker adorned with the righteousness of Jesus Christ.

They are the ones who will hear the Redeemer say, "Well done, thou good and faithful servant. Come, enter the joy of thy Lord."

[1]*Encyclopedia of 7700 Illustrations.*

Questions for Discussion

1. How is a life of sin like a cage?
2. How is being redeemed like a bird released from that cage?
3. Discuss the various meanings and uses of the word "redeemed" as used in Scripture.
4. What was the price paid for our redemption from the cage of sin?
5. What are the characteristics of the non-redeemed? the redeemed?
6. In the account of the Prodigal Son in Luke 15, what were his steps in becoming redeemed?
7. What is included in the power of the redeemed?

Questions submitted by
Elmer D. Glick
Kinzer, PA

CHAPTER 2

What Does the Bible Say? – Part 1

When reference is made to dress, clothing, and what one is going to wear, it often means conflict. Dad asks his son, "You are not going to church in those pants are you?" or Mom says to daughter, "You are not going to wear those clothes to go away tonight." As parents well know, there is often conflict between parents and children, young and older, on what to wear.

Is it only a parent-child problem? Or a young-versus-older problem? No, it's bigger than that. It is a conflict that began when Satan came to Adam and Eve in the garden of Eden. It is a spiritual battle in which Satan and the world have declared an all-out war on Christ and the church.

God created mankind in His own image. Then He said, "It is very good." God then set principles and boundaries in which mankind should live. The people who live voluntarily inside these boundaries are the ones who experience true contentment, purpose in living, and a deep abiding joy. Satan's strategy is to attack and discredit God, His principles, and those who follow the godly way of living. On the battlefront of dress principles, Satan wages a fierce war against God and the church of Jesus Christ.

The conflict over "what are you going to wear" is a conflict where the human heart is the battleground. Satan is in battle for control. The Holy Spirit urges you to turn your life over to Jesus Christ. As this conflict rages in the heart, it causes conflict in the home, in the church, in schools, and in the culture.

The globe is shrinking at an accelerated pace, often in ways unheard of before. Now a major event becomes a global television spectacular. Ideas, styles, and fads spread around the world, across once-formidable barriers, almost instantaneously. Some fad emerges on the other side of the globe, and within minutes it's flashed into American living rooms.

During the time when bobbed hair was becoming very fashionable, a southern governor did not want his girls to have bobbed hair. One day after school the governor's two teenage girls were pleading with their father for permission. One of the girls came out with the often-used remark, "But, Father, everybody's doing it."

The governor asked, "Whose daughters are you?" After hearing them acknowledge him, he said, "Sure. You are the daughters of the governor. You do not follow the styles. You *set* styles."[1]

The redeemed are the daughters and sons of the Redeemer. Do they follow the styles or do they set the styles?

The redeemed have found their redemption through the Scriptures. Faith comes by hearing the Word of God. It is the Bible that told them of their "robe of righteousness." The redeemed also get their directions on how to live and adorn themselves in their journey through life from the Bible.

Let us look at what the Bible says in relation to clothing, garments, and adornment.

> "And the LORD God said, It is not good that the man should be alone; I will make him an help meet for him. And out of the ground the LORD God formed every beast of the field, and every fowl of the air; and brought them unto Adam to see what he would call them: and whatsoever Adam called every living creature, that was the name thereof. And Adam gave names to all cattle, and to the fowl of the air, and to every beast of the field; but for Adam there was not found an help meet for him. And the LORD God caused a deep sleep to fall upon Adam, and he slept: and he took one of his ribs, and closed up the flesh instead thereof; and the rib, which the LORD God had taken from the man, made he a woman, and brought her unto the man. And Adam said, This is now bone of my bones, and flesh of my flesh: she shall be called Woman, because she was taken out of Man. Therefore shall a man leave his father and his mother, and shall cleave unto his wife: and they shall be one flesh. And they were both naked, the man and his wife, and were not ashamed" (Genesis 2:18-25).

God created Adam. Then God said it was not good for Adam to be alone. So He made a woman and brought her to Adam. They shall be one flesh.

> "And they were both naked, the man and his wife, and were not ashamed."

Here were two people living in an atmosphere of heaven, arrayed in innocence and glory. They had not sinned, and there was nothing to be ashamed of or to hide from. They were like innocent children without embarrassment or shame. Since there was no sin to cover, clothing was not yet introduced.

However, the picture changes.

> "Now the serpent was more subtil than any beast of the field which the LORD God had made. And he said unto the woman, Yea, hath God said, Ye shall not eat of every tree of the garden? And the woman said unto the serpent, We may eat of the fruit of the trees of the garden: but of the fruit of the tree which is in the midst of the garden, God hath said, Ye shall not eat of it, neither shall ye touch it, lest ye die. And the serpent said unto the woman, Ye shall not surely die: for God doth know that in the day ye eat thereof, then your eyes shall be opened, and ye shall be as gods, knowing good and evil. And when the woman saw that the tree was good for food, and that it was pleasant to the eyes, and a tree to be desired to make one wise, she took of the fruit thereof, and did eat, and gave also unto her husband with her: and he did eat. And the eyes of them both were opened, and they knew that they were naked; and they sewed fig leaves together, and made themselves aprons. And they heard the voice of the LORD God walking in the garden in the cool of the day: and Adam and his wife hid themselves from the presence of the LORD God amongst the trees of the garden. And the LORD God called unto Adam, and said unto him, Where art thou? And he said, I heard thy voice in the garden, and I was afraid, because I was naked; and I hid myself. And he said, Who told thee that thou wast naked? Hast thou eaten of the tree, whereof I commanded thee that thou shouldest not eat? And the man said, The woman whom thou gavest to be with me, she gave me of the tree, and I did eat" (Genesis 3:1-12).

Satan promised this couple that if they disobeyed God and ate the forbidden fruit they would know good and evil. They did sin. As the devil said, their eyes were opened, and they were no longer in innocence, but in guilt and shame. They knew they were naked before God.

This nakedness goes deeper than simply being without clothes and having the physical body exposed. They were now before God and exposed as described in Hebrews 4:13.

> "Neither is there any creature that is not manifest in his sight: but all things are naked and opened unto the eyes of him with whom we have to do."

God came walking in the garden looking for Adam. The Lord God called Adam and said, "Where are you?"

Adam answered: "I was afraid, because I was naked; and I hid myself."

Here are three significant words: afraid, naked, hid. Adam now became like a guilty child who has disobeyed. The sound of a parent coming into his presence brings on fear because of guilt in the heart.

Even dogs who have disobeyed their master give expressions of fear when their master catches them in the offense. Adam disobeyed. The sound of the Master brought fear. Adam was afraid. He also recognized he was naked. He was now exposed in *body* and *heart.* God sees to the very core of the heart. As the Bible says, "For the word of God is quick and powerful, and sharper than any two-edged sword, . . . a discerner of the thoughts and intents of the heart" (Hebrews 4:12).

Adam was now before the Lord with an exposed body, an exposed mind, and the very intents of the heart were naked before his Maker. No wonder he tried to hide.

When I was a schoolboy, one of my friends went with me to Aunt Emma's house, probably over the noon hour. For some reason we stopped by Uncle Red's sawmill before returning to school. Uncle Red's tractor had a belt connected to a wood saw. I was challenged to start up the engine on the tractor. I pushed the starter—the engine started and so did the saw. Within seconds, the belt spun off the pulley of the tractor. Oops! We had messed up something! We stopped the engine and got out of there. The next time Uncle Red and Aunt Emma came to spend the evening at our house, I did not run across the lawn to meet them as I usually did, but went to my parents bedroom to stay out of sight. I was afraid and didn't want to face them. So it was with Adam and Eve.

What could they do to hide their shame? They needed something to conceal and cover their sinfulness. God would be coming to meet them and they felt guilty about being fully exposed. So they tried to cover their shame. They sewed fig leaves together and made themselves apron-like girdles. These mini-skirts were not sufficient. Their self-made fig aprons were entirely inadequate.

Before God drove Adam and Eve from the garden, He made "coats of skins" and clothed them.

> "Unto Adam also and to his wife did the LORD God make coats of skins, and clothed them" (Genesis 3:21).

God provided a covering for their nakedness. Perhaps they watched guiltily and sorrowfully as God picked several of their friends, their sheep, and killed them before their eyes. Innocent blood was shed to obtain "coats of skins" to cover their shame.

What is so significant about "coats of skins"?

- Animals had to give up their lives to provide them.
- It required the shedding of innocent blood.
- It covered their bodies and physical shame.
- And it typified the coming of the spiritual Redeemer.

The "coats of skins" point to Jesus the perfect Redeemer. Jesus left heaven and came to earth. He gave His life and shed His innocent blood so you can have a "garment of salvation." The soldiers led Jesus to Golgotha. They tore off His robe from His bloody, mangled back and nailed Jesus to the cross to die. While Jesus was on the cross bearing your sin and shame, the soldiers were casting lots for His seamless, priestly robe that likely was made by His mother. Jesus Christ gave up His coat (tunic) so that when He comes again, you need not be caught in shame like Adam was in the garden, but you may have on a "robe of righteousness." He laid down His garment and took upon Himself your shame, so that you can have "the garment of praise" instead of a heavy spirit of fear.

The "coats of skins" were daily reminders to Adam and Eve of a coming Redeemer to cover their sins.

Why should you wear clothes? What could getting dressed mean to you? The wearing of clothing is a daily reminder of the need for the blood of Christ to cover your sins and give you the garment of salvation. Every day when you get dressed be reminded that Jesus Christ has redeemed you and purchased your robe of righteousness.

The wearing of clothing is a regular symbol of your need to be covered with salvation through Jesus

Christ. It also reminds us that when God sends Christ to meet His people, they must be wearing the wedding garment of righteousness.

What else does the Bible say about clothing and adornment?

> "The LORD also spoke to Moses, saying, "Speak to the sons of Israel, and tell them that they shall make for themselves tassels on the corners of their garments throughout their generations, and that they shall put on the tassel of each corner a cord of blue. And it shall be a tassel for you to look at and remember all the commandments of the LORD, so as to do them and not follow after your own heart and your own eyes, after which you played the harlot, in order that you may remember to do all my commandments, and be holy to your God. I am the LORD your God who brought you out from the land of Egypt to be your God; I am the LORD your God" (Numbers 15:37-41, NASV).

God told Moses to instruct the Israelites to make tassels with a blue cord in each tassel. They were to fasten them to the corners of their garments. As they would walk along the tassels would swirl at the edge of the garment.

What was the purpose of the tassels with a blue ribbon or cord in each tassel?

It was a distinctive identification of God's people. They were there to remind Israel who they were. They were to be worn as reminders of God's commands. They were obedience reminders. As these tassels with the ribbon of blue were worn, it reminded them to obey God's commands rather than following the lustful desires of their hearts. It was a daily reminder to obey all the commandments of God rather than chasing after what their eyes wanted.

When the Israelites got dressed for the day, these tassels were there reminding them of who they were and reminding them to obey all of God's commands. Should there be something about the attire of the redeemed to remind them of who they are, and to remind them to fully obey the will of the Redeemer?

Here is another principle in Scripture:

> "The woman shall not wear that which pertaineth unto a man, neither shall a man put on a woman's garment: for all that do so are abomination unto the LORD thy God" (Deuteronomy 22:5).

This command calls for a clear male-female distinction. It calls for men to wear masculine clothing. Women's clothing is to be feminine. Women who wear men's clothing or men who wear women's are an abomination to God. Unisex fashion, garments, or hairstyles are outside of the will of God.

Some may say this is an Old Testament command. I find nowhere in the entire Bible that God changed His mind on this issue. In fact, the New Testament calls for male-female distinction with the woman's uncut hair and the man's shorn hair. The redeemed—those who wear the garment of salvation—should wear clothing that leaves no question of gender.

I know we are living in a culture that promotes unisex clothing and hairstyling. Years ago when long hair on men began to appear I was at a meeting with a friend where hundreds of Christians were gathered. We sat behind a person who had long hair and wore trousers. I asked my friend, "What is it?" We did not know for sure whether it was a man or a woman.

There is a story about a French student who traveled through Europe with a false photograph on his passport. He was never stopped, even though the photograph was of his cocker spaniel. Said a red-faced border official: "It's the way kids wear their hair these days."[2]

I say again, the redeemed—those with the garment of salvation—should wear clothing that leaves no question of gender.

During Old Testament times, before the birth of Jesus Christ, God promised to meet with His people at the tabernacle. A priest was responsible for making animal sacrifices "for his own sins as well as for the sins of the people" (Hebrews 5:3). Day after day the priest performed his duties in offering sacrifices.

The priests were instructed to wear priestly garments to enter the tabernacle. So each day the priest wore his uniform to go to the tabernacle. The office, dress, and ministration of the high priest were typical of the priesthood of our Lord (our Redeemer).

God gave Moses detailed instructions on making the priestly garments (Exodus 28). The garments were to be made of gold, blue, purple, and scarlet yarn, "and fine twined linen" (Exodus 28:6). These priestly garments were of such precise and detailed order that God called special people and endowed them with special skills to make them. Woven into the details of the garments were symbols pointing to Jesus Christ, our Redeemer.

Exodus 39 records their obedience in making the holy garments. They used blue, purple, and red thread to make clothes for the priests. They made a robe of blue to be worn under the holy vest.

Ervin Hershberger wrote, "this Robe of Blue pointed to the Heavenly Prince, the coming 'KING of Kings.'"[3] I suspect it may have been seamless like the coat of Jesus.

> "Then the soldiers, when they had crucified Jesus, took his garments, and made four parts, to every soldier a part; and also his coat: now the coat was without seam, woven from the top throughout" (John 19:23).

The priest was to wear a turban with a plate of gold tied to it, having this inscription: HOLINESS TO THE LORD.

When the priest went to the tabernacle to worship God and make sacrifices, he was to meet God in a priestly garment. Not just any kind of clothing was acceptable.

Is there a lesson to be learned? How shall we dress to gather in worship to God? Will just anything do?

Let's look again at the prodigal son who left the hogpen and returned to his father. The son came to his senses and saw his foolishness. He went back to his father and said, "Father, I have sinned against heaven, and in thy sight, and am no more worthy to be called thy son." The father called for the best robe and put it upon his son. Then they killed the fatted calf, made a feast, and celebrated.

The best robe on the prodigal son was the father's expression of forgiveness. It was a festive robe of honor that covered the scars of the hogpen and indicated that the son was redeemed! The robe was an essential part of this redemption celebration.

God is waiting to meet any sinner who comes to his senses, repents of the hogpen of sin, and returns to the Father. The sinner doesn't need to stop and change clothes when he leaves the hogpen to come to God. The sinner can come to God straight out of the mire of sin. God accepts the sinner as he is.

However, when the sinner comes to God in true repentance saying, "I have sinned against heaven," and seeks forgiveness, that person is granted forgiveness through the blood of Jesus Christ. That person is redeemed and receives a garment of salvation.

It would have been most disrespectful for the prodigal son to insist on wearing his dirty, stinky hog-pen clothes to his father's celebration. The son went to the feast in the best robe.

The priests needed to dress up to meet God. They dressed in garments that had symbolic meaning. Wouldn't it seem reasonable then that the redeemed who have a clean garment of salvation would want to "dress up" to assemble for public worship of the Redeemer? Should not the redeemed use care in selecting garments that do not symbolize the hogpen? Shouldn't their garments symbolize the new life, the new robe, and honor the Redeemer?

[1]*Encyclopedia of 7700 Illustrations.*
[2]*Encyclopedia of 7700 Illustrations.*
[3]*Seeing Christ in the Tabernacle.* Ervin Hershberger.

Questions for Discussion

Genesis 3:20-21

1. Why were the fig leaves which Adam and Eve sewed together inadequate?

2. Consider carefully that the Creator made the coats of skins. What kind of finish quality did these coats possess?

3. How were the "coats of skins" superior to the the man-sewn fig leaves in providing for modesty?

Genesis 35:1-8

4. What is the significance in the removal of the jewelry and the changing of clothes by Jacob and his family before going to Bethel to worship the Lord?

Numbers 15:37-41

5. God prescribed a distinguishing mark for His people in the Old Testament that set them apart from the world. How does this principle apply to the people of God today? *See Romans 12:2 (conformed) and 1 Peter 1:14 (fashioned). Look up the original Greek meaning for these words.*

Matthew 6:10

6. "Thy will be done *in earth* as it is *in heaven.*" It is safe to conclude that all the inhabitants of heaven are in full compliance with the will of God. What bearing does this verse have on His children on earth?

Questions submitted by
Eldwin Campbell
Dayton, VA

CHAPTER 3

What Does the Bible Say? – Part 2

When searching the Scripture to find what it says about dress and outward adorning, one should not miss 2 Kings 9:30.

> "And when Jehu was come to Jezreel, Jezebel heard of it; and she painted her face, and tired her head, and looked out at a window" (2 Kings 9:30).

The reference here is to the woman Jezebel. She has stamped her name in history as the representative of all that is evil, malicious, and revengeful. She promoted idolatry of the most debased and sensual kind. She was the first instigator of severe persecution against the people of God. She was the epitome of wickedness.

Her name came to be used as the synonym, or symbol, of a wicked woman. The old Apostle John was abandoned by man on the Isle of Patmos. There God called John to write in a book the visions He would show him about the seven churches. In Revelation chapter two he records what he saw in the church of Thyatira.

"And unto the angel of the church in Thyatira write; These things saith the Son of God, who hath his eyes like unto a flame of fire, and his feet are like fine brass; I know thy works, and charity, and service, and faith, and thy patience, and thy works; and the last to be more than the first. Notwithstanding I have a few things against thee, because thou sufferest that woman Jezebel, which calleth herself a prophetess, to teach and to seduce my servants to commit fornication, and to eat things sacrificed unto idols" (Revelation 2:18-20).

In this passage God inserted the name Jezebel. This wicked Jezebel of the Thyatira church taught the acts of adultery and sexual immorality contrary to the rules of the Jerusalem council recorded in Acts 15:29. She wins "the gold" for wickedness (be aware, gold also perishes under the judgment of God).

What does this wicked woman have to do with external practices of appearance? Why is her name mentioned in relation to the attire of the redeemed?

Because "Jezebel is the perfect example of the external practices corresponding to the internal character."[1] The Bible explains that she painted her face, she fixed her hair, and "adorned her head."[2] Jezebel plastered on the makeup and fixed up her hair. Her outward adornment was a reflection of her wicked heart. Her adornment symbolized her wickedness.

Jesus indicted the ministers of the Thyatira church for tolerating Jezebel. He said, "I have a few things against thee. You tolerate Jezebel's teaching and leading my bond servants astray." Jesus warned the church leaders about the spirit of Jezebelism in the church. What would He say to the churches today where they pull out the hymnbook and sing, "I will sing of my

Redeemer . . ." if the words are coming from painted lips that are encased in "made-up" faces, topped with expensive hairdo's and jewelry dangling from their ears? I believe the message would be similar to the one for the Thyatira church—repent! If you claim redemption, then do not wear any symbols of Jezebel's wickedness.

Another Scripture that gives some guidance to the redeemed on attire is Isaiah 3:16 through 4:1.

> "Moreover the Lord saith, Because the daughters of Zion are haughty, and walk with stretched forth necks and wanton eyes, walking and mincing as they go, and making a tinkling with their feet: therefore the Lord will smite with a scab the crown of the head of the daughters of Zion, and the LORD will discover their secret parts. In that day the Lord will take away the bravery of their tinkling ornaments about their feet, and their cauls, and their round tires like the moon, the chains, and the bracelets, and the mufflers, the bonnets, and the ornaments of the legs, and the headbands, and the tablets, and the earrings, the rings, and nose jewels, the changeable suits of apparel, and the mantles, and the wimples, and the crisping pins, the glasses, and the fine linen, and the hoods, and the vails. And it shall come to pass, that instead of sweet smell there shall be stink; and instead of a girdle a rent; and instead of well set hair baldness; and instead of a stomacher a girding of sackcloth; and burning instead of beauty. Thy men shall fall by the sword, and thy mighty in the war. And her gates shall lament and mourn; and she being desolate shall sit upon the ground. And in that day seven women shall take hold of one man, saying, We will eat our own bread, and wear our own apparel: only let us be called by thy name, to take away our reproach" (Isaiah 3:16-4:1).

Isaiah was sent by God to warn Israel of their departure from obeying God's laws. God had clearly instructed them that obedience will bring His blessing upon them. He also had warned them that if they were not careful to observe the words of the Law, then the Lord would send judgment. God forewarned them that disobedience would cause Him to bring a fierce nation, who would have no respect for the old or young, that would besiege their land and carry out judgment. These forewarnings are clearly recorded in the book of Deuteronomy, chapter 28.

Israel was not careful to obey God's Law. Isaiah faithfully reminded the people of the consequences of disobedience, warned them of judgment, and gave them opportunities to change their ways. In this third chapter of Isaiah the people are warned that Jehovah God stands ready to judge the people. The judgment is directed toward the elders and princes, the people who were in ruling and leadership positions.

Suddenly the prophet changes focus from censoring the rulers. In verse 16 he begins with a lightning-like bolt of judgment against the proud and haughty women of Jerusalem. These proud and haughty women contribute to the corruption and fall of Judah.

> "Moreover the Lord saith, Because the daughters of Zion are haughty, and walk with stretched forth necks and wanton eyes, walking and mincing as they go, and making a tinkling with their feet" (Isaiah 3:16).

The way women conduct their lives has a tremendous force in making or breaking a nation. Jehovah God has charged these women with being haughty, proud, and arrogant. They seek attention by the way they walk and the trinkets they wear. The prophet lists twenty-one items prized by the women of the day,

35

from anklets to various garments of ornamentation. Isaiah sees the selfish, proud, and sensuous lives of these women patterned after the pagan world with its lusts and lascivious ways. He warns them that the sexual features which they use to draw attention will be laid bare in shame and humiliation by crude and barbarous captors.

Preacher Bill Burkett wrote, "After reading what Isaiah says about externalism, let no Christian ever say that externalism is of no concern to God or that it has no moral consequence."[3]

The modern day interpreters find a way to weave into their comments the idea that it is not the excessive adorning that is against God's will, but the proud hearts. I find it difficult to read this passage with an open mind and not get a sense that with God both go together. The outward show is a display of a haughty and proud heart. To become redeemed means becoming humble. How can those who through a humble and contrite heart become children of God rise from their confession of Christ and bedeck themselves with ornaments that go with pride? Since humility is a requirement for being redeemed, how can those who profess redemption continue to pattern their outward adornment after the world? Profession of redemption and worldly attire are an abomination to God.

Next I draw attention to a passage from the Prophet Zephaniah. He was God's prophetic voice of judgment and horrible punishment for all who would defy the Lord. He warned of God's wrath that would sweep away everything in the land and destroy it. Destruction was coming because Judah had forsaken the Lord.

"I will utterly consume all things from off the land, saith the LORD. I will consume man and beast; I will consume the fowls of the heaven, and the fishes of the sea, and the stumblingblocks with the wicked; and I will cut off man from off the land, saith the LORD. I will also stretch out mine hand upon Judah, and upon all the inhabitants of Jerusalem; and I will cut off the remnant of Baal from this place, and the name of the Chemarims with the priests; and them that worship the host of heaven upon the housetops; and them that worship and that swear by the LORD, and that swear by Malcham; and them that are turned back from the LORD; and those that have not sought the LORD, nor enquired for him. Hold thy peace at the presence of the Lord GOD: for the day of the LORD is at hand: for the LORD hath prepared a sacrifice, he hath bid his guests. And it shall come to pass in the day of the Lord's sacrifice, that I will punish the princes, and the king's children, and all such as are clothed with strange apparel" (Zephaniah 1:2-8).

Look at the context of this coming judgment.

- I will sweep away everything from the face of the earth.
- The wicked will have only heaps of rubble.
- I will stretch out my hand against Judah.
- I will destroy those who turn away from the Lord.

In verse 8 He includes punishment for all those in worldly clothing.

"I will punish . . . all such as are clothed with strange apparel" (KJV).

"I will punish . . . all who clothe themselves in foreign garments" (NASV).

"And on the day of the Lord's sacrifice I will punish the officials and the king's sons, and all who are clothed in [lavish] foreign apparel (instead of the Jewish dress, with its reminders to obey God's commandments)" (Numbers 15:38, 39, Amplified).

One of the things Judah did that displeased God and contributed to judgment and punishment was the wearing of foreign worldly clothes.

The argument is often made that God doesn't care how we dress. He looks on the heart and not outward appearance. That argument runs counter to this passage of Scripture. Numbers 15:38, 39 records specific instructions from God on attire for His people. Judah did not follow these instructions. Instead they wore pagan clothes which showed their desire for foreign ways and false gods. God's Word tells us that He does care. It makes it clear that instead of bringing on God's blessing, this practice contributed to the coming of judgment and punishment.

> "Speak unto the children of Israel, and bid them that they make them fringes in the borders of their garments throughout their generations, and that they put upon the fringe of the borders a ribband of blue: and it shall be unto you for a fringe, that ye may look upon it, and remember all the commandments of the LORD, and do them; and that ye seek not after your own heart and your own eyes, after which ye use to go a whoring" (Numbers 15:38, 39).

Jesus draws attention to the lifestyle of a selfish rich man. "The rich man died and was buried; and in hell he lifted up his eyes, being in torment" (Luke 16:19). This man lived in the luxury of expensive clothing, extravagant feasting, and merry splendor every day. It wasn't the riches and fine clothes that condemned the man, was it? Wasn't it his selfish heart? That may be true, but it was his selfish heart that drove him to costly clothes and lavish living. He heaped this on himself and let the poor go hungry. In true reality, selfishness, expressed with lavish living and costly clothing, does not fit the life of the redeemed.

From these passages of Scripture, 2 Kings, Revelation, Isaiah, Zephaniah, and Luke, emerges the picture of wickedness and pride that is boldly expressed by outward adornment. The wickedness of the heart is symbolized by paint, jewelry, the fixing of the hair, and the refusal to wear the garments God prescribed for His people.

It takes a lot of anxious thought and careful trifling to be adorned with makeup and jewelry.

Jesus taught His followers to not be anxious and worried about their lives, their bodies, or about food and clothes.

"Therefore I say unto you, Take no thought for your life, what ye shall eat, or what ye shall drink; nor yet for your body, what ye shall put on. Is not the life more than meat, and the body than raiment? Behold the fowls of the air: for they sow not, neither do they reap, nor gather into barns; yet your heavenly Father feedeth them. Are ye not much better than they? Which of you by taking thought can add one cubit unto his stature? And why take ye thought for raiment? Consider the lilies of the field, how they grow; they toil not, neither do they spin: and yet I say unto you, That even Solomon in all his glory was not arrayed like one of these. Wherefore, if God so clothe the grass of the field, which to day is, and tomorrow is cast into the oven, shall he not much more clothe you, O ye of little faith? Therefore take no thought, saying, What shall we eat? or, What shall we drink? or, Wherewithal shall we be clothed? (For after all these things do the Gentiles seek:) for your heavenly Father knoweth that ye have need of all these things. But seek ye first the kingdom of God, and his righteousness; and all these things shall be added unto you. Take therefore no thought for the morrow: for the morrow shall take thought for the things of itself. Sufficient unto the day is the evil thereof" (Matthew 6:25-34).

How does this passage speak to the attire of the redeemed? The Scriptures we looked at pictured persons giving anxious care to adorning themselves. Here Jesus implies that the Gentiles, the heathen, worry about what they will eat, drink, and wear. He said, "For all these things the Gentiles eagerly seek." They crave and diligently seek after *things*. The heathen give much thought and consideration to being dressed according to the world's fashion. The redeemed can be completely free from this kind of worry. The redeemed need not give any thought to what is in style and what is not.

Jesus refers to clothing the second time in His "Sermon on the Mount."

"Beware of false prophets, which come to you in sheep's clothing, but inwardly they are ravening wolves" (Matthew 7:15).

Jesus warns His followers to beware of false prophets. The false prophets will be used by Satan in an attempt to deceive the very elect. One of the ways of deception will be to come in sheep's clothing. Jesus is sounding the warning of a person who is a hypocrite in heart. The very core of a false prophet's *will and heart is not* with Jesus Christ. Jesus further warns that this kind of person will come to you in sheep's clothing. The meaning of the word clothing is simple. It means just that: clothing, garment, raiment, the outer robe. These false prophets may have been persons who were anti-Christ in heart, but outwardly donned the prescribed garment for God's people with the "fringe in the borders" and the "cord of blue" (Numbers 15:37-41). Today we have plenty of false teachers who hide behind the "clergy garb" or the "clergy collar."

Jesus referred to sheep and sheep's clothing. In Jesus' teachings He referred to "my sheep," or "the sheep," etc. His reference to sheep is speaking of the redeemed. Those who have repented of their sins and yielded their will and lives to Him are His sheep. He then refers to "sheep's clothing." The false prophets come "dressed as sheep" (Amplified). The reference to "sheep's clothing" gives the idea that sheep—the redeemed—will be known for who they are by their clothing. There is such a thing as sheep's clothing.

Since Jesus referred to "sheep's clothing," what might that mean for the redeemed sheep?

We continue to look at what the Bible says about the attire of the redeemed.

> "Now I praise you, brethren, that ye remember me in all things, and keep the ordinances, as I delivered them to you. But I would have you know, that the head of every man is Christ; and the head of the woman is the man; and the head of Christ is God. Every man praying or prophesying, having his head covered, dishonoureth his head. But every woman that prayeth or prophesieth with her head uncovered dishonoureth her head: for that is even all one as if she were shaven. For if the woman be not covered, let her also be shorn: but if it be a shame for a woman to be shorn or shaven, let her be covered. For a man indeed ought not to cover his head, forasmuch as he is the image and glory of God: but the woman is the glory of the man. For the man is not of the woman; but the woman of the man. Neither was the man created for the woman; but the woman for the man. For this cause ought

41

the woman to have power on her head because of the angels. Nevertheless neither is the man without the woman, neither the woman without the man, in the Lord. For as the woman is of the man, even so is the man also by the woman; but all things of God. Judge in yourselves: is it comely that a woman pray unto God uncovered? Doth not even nature itself teach you, that, if a man have long hair, it is a shame unto him? But if a woman have long hair, it is a glory to her: for her hair is given her for a covering. But if any man seem to be contentious, we have no such custom, neither the churches of God" (1 Corinthians 11:2-16).

This passage affirms and strengthens the headship order that was established at Creation. It gives instructive principles on how redeemed men and women should wear their hair. As an act of obedience to God and a daily reminder to ourselves of God's principle of order, the woman is to wear long hair and a covering. The man is not to have long hair, and he is not to wear a symbolic covering. This Scripture reinforces the teaching that the redeemed should wear clothing that leaves no question of gender identification.

The attire of the redeemed.

"I will therefore that men pray every where, lifting up holy hands, without wrath and doubting. In like manner also, that women adorn themselves in modest apparel, with shamefacedness and sobriety; not with broided hair, or gold, or pearls, or costly array. But (which becometh women professing godliness) with good works" (1 Timothy 2:8-10).

Paul's instruction here is connected to the subject of godliness. This instructs women to be modest and sensible about their clothes. One meaning given for modesty is "bashfulness toward men and awe toward God." "The word denotes feminine reserve in matters of sex." "Shamefacedness" signifies that modesty which steps back from overstepping the limits of womanly reserve. Today there are many careless women who seem to have no sense of shame or reserve toward others, or men, and in how they expose their bodies. This is a call to decency and godliness in clothing.

Sobriety calls for sanity or self control. These ideals are upheld by avoiding fancy hairstyles, gold ornaments, pearls, jewelry, and expensive dresses. Peter confirms what Paul taught. He gives us the mind of the Spirit on the same subject which agrees with Paul's letter to Timothy.

> "Likewise, ye wives, be in subjection to your own husbands; that, if any obey not the word, they also may without the word be won by the conversation of the wives; while they behold your chaste conversation coupled with fear. Whose adorning let it not be that outward adorning of plaiting the hair, and of wearing of gold, or of putting on of apparel; but let it be the hidden man of the heart, in that which is not corruptible, even the ornament of a meek and quiet spirit, which is in the sight of God of great price. For after this manner in the old time the holy women also, who trusted in God, adorned themselves, being in subjection unto their own husbands" (1 Peter 3:1-5).

Peter is addressing the subject of adorning the outward appearance. His instruction pertains to moral behavior and chastity. The word *chaste* means modest and pure. "Purity means to be free from impurities. A woman cannot be pure if she is practicing the worldly arts. She is not pure if there is vanity, extravagance or any other form of worldliness in the heart."[4]

There are four things the Bible is asking godly women to avoid.

1. Outward adorning. The Scripture calls for redeemed sisters to avoid the outward worldly adornment or decoration.

2. Dying the hair, "hairdos," and the worldly practice of broidering the hair with brightly colored materials that was the custom of the day.

3. Wearing of gold, putting on jewelry.

4. Expensive and fine clothing.

Instead of these outward put-ons, the Christian woman is to cultivate the inner beauty of a gentle and peaceful spirit. Her beauty should reveal the peace and joy that comes from the work of redemption in her heart. She should not decorate herself in a way that draws the attention to herself instead of to the work of grace in her heart.

The Scriptures and attire.

> "And I turned to see the voice that spake with me. And being turned, I saw seven golden candlesticks; and in the midst of the seven candlesticks one like unto the Son of man, *clothed with a garment down to the foot*, and girt about the paps with a golden girdle. His head and his hairs were white like wool, as white as snow; and his eyes were as a flame of fire; and his feet like unto fine brass, as if they burned in a furnace; and his voice as the sound of many waters" (Revelation 1:12-15).

The Apostle John lived with Jesus during His short ministry on earth. He saw Jesus Christ in everyday life as they traveled together. He ate with Jesus, saw Jesus perform miracles, heal the sick, and cast out devils.

John became the best friend of Jesus. His friendship took John right to the foot of the cross. From the cross Jesus spoke to John. John saw Jesus after the soldiers stripped him of his garments and nailed him to the cross where he hung in open shame and paid the price of redemption. Now the old Apostle John sees Jesus again. He heard a voice and turned to see the voice that spoke with him. He saw seven golden candlesticks, and in the midst of the candlesticks he saw one like unto the Son of man. He again saw the Lord Jesus Christ.

I can imagine the Apostle John had many images of Jesus deeply imbedded in his mind. Perhaps he had the memory of Jesus taking the Twelve up into a mountain for their ordination where He ordained them to be with Him and to go forth and preach. He probably didn't erase the scene of Jesus taking five dinner buns and two fishes, looking up to heaven, blessing the food, and feeding about five thousand. Neither did he forget Jesus on the cross. This time, when he turned and looked, there was Jesus. This time He was clothed with a robe that reached to His feet. He had a golden sash around His chest. His head and hair were white as snow. A sharp two-edged sword came out of His mouth. He looked like the sun shining at its brightest.

When John saw Him, he fell at His feet like a dead man. Jesus laid His right hand on John and said, "I am the first and the last. I am the one who lives. I was dead. But look, I am alive forever and ever" (Revelation 1:17b-18a, NCV).

Since we are looking at the subject of attire for the redeemed, I draw attention to the mention in this wonderful passage that Jesus was clothed in a robe that came to the foot.

Redeemed men, take the example of your Redeemer when you go out on your job, mow the yard, wash the car, go to the mountain or on vacation—leave your shirts on and wear trousers that cover to the foot. Attire for the redeemed means attire that covers the body and symbolizes your need for Christ's garment of salvation.

What might sheep's clothing mean for the redeemed?

> "Because thou sayest, I am rich, and increased with goods, and have need of nothing; and knowest not that thou art wretched, and miserable, and poor, and blind, and naked: I counsel thee to buy of me gold tried in the fire, that thou mayest be rich; and white raiment, that thou mayest be clothed, and that the shame of thy naked-ness do not appear; and anoint thine eyes with eyesalve, that thou mayest see" (Revelation 3:17, 18).

I referred to this Scripture in chapter 1, *Who Are the Redeemed?* I will briefly refer to it again.

The Laodicean church was wealthy. Their city was known for manufacturing fine, glossy clothes, proba-bly the finest clothes money could buy. In spite of their clothing industry, God counseled them:
• you need the white robes of salvation.
• you stand spiritually naked before me.
• you are invited to take the garment of salvation.

> "Behold, I come as a thief. Blessed is he that watch-eth, and keepeth his garments, lest he walk naked, and they see his shame" (Revelation 16:15).

These two passages point to our spiritual garments

given to us by Christ. Putting clothes on your physical body is a daily symbol that your spiritual shame needs to be covered with the robe of righteousness given to you by Christ.

Since physical clothing symbolizes your need for spiritual clothing, should the redeemed then exercise care that their clothing does not distort the symbol of salvation? I believe they should!

This is why I am convinced that sports symbols, silly sayings, foolish and morally loose art, gaudy colors, and other distractions do not belong on the garments of the redeemed. The sheep's clothing should not be cluttered with the paraphernalia that matches with the wolves and the goats. I believe it dishonors our Redeemer when believers wear insignias that belong to the world.

In looking at what the Bible says about attire and what sheep's clothing might mean for the redeemed, we give attention to two passages in Revelation. First, Revelation 17:1-6. Here we look at "THE MOTHER OF HARLOTS."

> "And there came one of the seven angels which had the seven vials, and talked with me, saying unto me, Come hither; I will shew unto thee the judgment of the great whore that sitteth upon many waters: with whom the kings of the earth have committed fornication, and the inhabitants of the earth have been made drunk with the wine of her fornication. So he carried me away in the spirit into the wilderness: and I saw a woman sit upon a scarlet coloured beast, full of names of blasphemy, having seven heads and ten horns. And the woman was arrayed in purple and scarlet colour, and decked with gold and precious stones and pearls, having a golden cup in her hand full of abominations and filthiness of her for-

nication: and upon her forehead was a name written, MYSTERY, BABYLON THE GREAT, THE MOTHER OF HARLOTS AND ABOMINATIONS OF THE EARTH. And I saw the woman drunken with the blood of the saints, and with the blood of the martyrs of Jesus: and when I saw her, I wondered with great admiration" (Revelation 17:1-6).

Solomon warns young men about prostitutes. Look out for the woman who is dressed as a prostitute. She is out to trick you, young man! She is known by her attire.

And, behold, there met him a woman with the attire of an harlot, and subtil of heart" (Proverbs 7:10).

How does a prostitute look? How does she dress? God told us in this Revelation passage. Here is a description of the wife of the devil, the counterfeit church, and what she looks like.

She is riding a bright red beast. This beast "was covered with names against God written on him." This beast was covered with blasphemous insignias against God and in honor of the devil.

The mother of prostitutes was dressed in dazzling purple and bright red. She was glittering with gold, jewels, and precious pearls. She held a cup in her hand that was filled with the abominable offenses and the filth of her immorality. And she is drunk! "She is drunk with the blood of those who were killed because of their faith in Jesus" (Revelation 17:6, NCV).

What's the meaning of purple and scarlet? From *Word Meanings in the New Testament* come the following observations:

"In the prophets scarlet is often linked with ungodly and sinful conduct. Purple and pomp, the worldly pomp of the demonic power Babylon in Revelation. The woman sits on a scarlet beast, . . . and she is herself arrayed in purple and scarlet.

"Only purple and scarlet fit the deeds of this woman, namely licentiousness, seduction by wine of unchastity, blasphemies, abomination, and murder of the witnesses of Jesus. Here red epitomizes demonic abomination, ungodly lasciviousness and the power which is hostile to God."[5]

J. B. Smith, a Mennonite scholar of Revelation, wrote this about the Great Harlot:

"Here is the height of adornment and at the same time the depth of corruption. The more the church loses her sense of inward values which 'in the sight of God are of great price,' the more she seeks to atone for this loss by adorning the outward man. It has always been so."[6]

What happens to the prostitute?

"She will be destroyed by fire, because the Lord who judges her is powerful."

"All your rich and fancy things have disappeared. You will never have them again." Terrible! How terrible for the great city! She was dressed in fine linen and purple cloth. She was shining with gold, jewels, pearls! "All these riches have been destroyed in one hour" (Revelation 18:8, 14, 16, 17, NCV).

"Therefore shall her plagues come in one day, death, and mourning, and famine; and she shall be utterly burned with fire: for strong is the Lord God who judgeth her. . . . And the fruits that thy soul lusted after are departed from thee, and all things which were dainty and goodly are departed from thee, and thou shalt find them no more at all. . . . And saying, Alas, alas that great city, that was clothed in fine linen, and purple, and scarlet, and decked with gold, and precious stones, and pearls! For in one hour so great riches is come to nought. And every shipmaster, and all the company of ships, and sailors, and as many as trade by sea, stood afar off" (Revelation 18:8, 14, 16, 17, NCV).

Listen, friends! The prostitute is condemned to hell. Her attire represents wickedness and doom. Let me assure you that this redeemed child of God will not show up wearing a scarlet red shirt or with a dazzling purple suit. I do not want to be caught wearing the color of harlots and the selfish rich man who lifted up his eyes in hell.

Now, turn to a very exciting passage in Revelation. Revelation 19:1-9:

"And after these things I heard a great voice of much people in heaven, saying, Alleluia; Salvation, and glory, and honour, and power, unto the Lord our God: for true and righteous are his judgments: for he hath judged the great whore, which did corrupt the earth with her fornication, and hath avenged the blood of his servants at her hand. And again they said, Alleluia. And her smoke rose up for ever and ever. And the four and twenty elders and the four beasts fell down and worshipped God that sat on the throne, saying, Amen; Alleluia. And a voice came out of the throne, saying, Praise our God, all ye his servants, and ye that fear him, both small and great. And I heard as it were the voice of a great multitude, and as the voice of many waters, and as the voice of mighty thunderings, saying, Alleluia: for the Lord God omnipotent reigneth. Let us be glad and rejoice, and give honour to him: for the marriage of the Lamb is come, and his wife hath made herself ready. And to her was granted that she should be arrayed in fine linen, clean and white: for the fine linen is the righteousness of saints. And he saith unto me, Write, Blessed are they which are called unto the marriage supper of the Lamb. And he saith unto me, These are the true sayings of God" (Revelation 19:1-9).

John heard what sounded like the roar of a great multitude of people in heaven. They were praising God by saying, "Hallelujah! Salvation, glory, and power belong to our God!"

"His judgments are true and right."

"Our God has condemned and punished this evil prostitute. He punished her for corrupting the earth with her immorality. God punished her because she killed His servants!" Again they shouted, "Hallelujah!"

> "She is burning, and her smoke will rise forever and ever" (Revelation 19:3, NCV).

Then John heard what sounded like a great multitude of people. It reminded him of the roar of flooding waters and loud peals of thunder. And this multitude was saying, "Hallelujah!"

"Our Lord God, the Almighty reigns and rules."

"He is the all powerful!"

"Let us be glad and rejoice, and give honor to him!"

What's all the rejoicing and shouting about?

The prostitute has been judged and the wedding of the Lamb has come. This is the great marriage of Jesus Christ and His bride. Redemption—deliverance has been completed. His bride has made herself ready. Ready! Yes, she was in her wedding garment. She was given fine, radiant linen that was bright and clean. This fine linen will not be cotton, nylon or double knit. Perhaps the Psalmist's words capture the meaning of these new wedding garments:

> "Bless the LORD, O my soul. O LORD my God, thou art very great; thou art clothed with honour and majesty.

Who coverest thyself with light as with a garment: who stretchest out the heavens like a curtain" (Psalm 104:1, 2).

"As for me, I will behold thy face in righteousness: I shall be satisfied, when I awake, with thy likeness" (Psalm 17:15).

The bride "will greatly rejoice in the Lord," her "soul shall be joyful" in her God. For He has clothed her "with the garments of salvation," and has covered her "with the robe of righteousness" (Isaiah 61:10).

At this marriage supper of the Lamb the bride will be clothed with linen. This fine linen signifies the righteousness of the saints. It represents their right standing before God, their righteous living, their godly conduct, and those good deeds they did for others as unto Christ. Isaiah wrote about "the robe of righteousness." The fine linen of the marriage supper represents righteousness. There are many people in this world who profess Jesus Christ, but their lives do not produce righteousness. Much of their lifestyle is a reflection of the great harlot. Will they be at the marriage supper in robes of righteousness? It seems to me the Bible is clear that a profession without fruit is dead.

There is a sharp contrast between the array of the Bride and the great harlot. One is arrayed in "fine linen, clean and white," the other in purple and scarlet, decked with gold and expensive stones. The Bride will be eternally rejoicing with Jesus. The harlot will be eternally tormented in the smoke of her wickedness.

Those who are willing to live disciplined lives for Jesus on this sinful earth will be rewarded with fine, spotless linen for all eternity. It will be a robe that covers all the scars of the "hogpen."

Those who try to have their heaven now, with their

fine linen here, will have it go up in smoke and be eternally in shame without a covering for sin.

Purple in the Scriptures is the royal color. It stands for The Royal One. Purple was also the color worn by the rich and those in royal positions. The selfish rich man clothed himself in purple and lived lavishly. The mother of harlots used this expensive purple dyed fabric to draw attention to herself. When Jesus Christ stood on trial before Pilate, Pilate ordered Jesus to be scourged. After the scourging that tore the back of Jesus to shreds, they put a purple robe on His bloody back and a crown of thorns on His head. Then they took something like sticks and clubbed Him on the head and spit on Him. They bowed down before Him saying "Hail, King of the Jews." The purple robe, the crown, and the bowing down was genuine mockery.

That purple robe of mockery reminds me that Jesus stood before Pilate and gave Himself to become your ransom for sin. He accepted that purple robe of mockery so that sinful and selfish purple "robers" can be redeemed. He allowed them to torture Him and then yank the purple robe off His mangled back and then nail Him to the cross where He died.

Why did Jesus allow this? So that when you stand trial before God, you can have more than a fake purple robe. You can have a robe of righteousness, "clean and white," and you will not need to be led away to be scourged and then cast into everlasting perdition with the devil. Instead, you'll be at the marriage supper of Jesus with a robe clean and bright that has no stain or odor from the "pigpen of sin." "Though your sins be as scarlet, they shall be as white as snow" (Isaiah 1:18). What shall the redeemed do with these teachings from the Word of God? Wearing of clothes is a symbol of our need for the garment of salvation.

- Clothing is to be gender distinctive.
- It is to remind us of godliness.
- It is to be modest.
- It is to reflect humility.
- It is to mirror the inner beauty of Jesus within you.

The starting point is this: by an act of your repentant will, invite Jesus Christ into the wardrobe of your heart. Then invite His Spirit to walk with you into your physical wardrobe. Invite Him to point out clothing that does not meet the teaching of His Word. Then invite Him to join you at the sewing machine to be careful to design your clothing in a manner that exalts Him over yourself. Invite Him to guide you as you stroll the malls and to give you the will power to walk on past anything that would be inconsistent with your robe of righteousness. Invite Him to guide you to buy nothing that dishonors His great name.

Questions for Discussion

[1] The Hargios Letter #7490.
[2] NAS.
[3] The Hargios Letter #7490.
[4] *Ibid*.
[5] Ralph Earle, *Word Meanings in the New Testament*. Baker Book House.
[6] J. B. Smith, *A Revelation of Jesus Christ*. Herald Press 1961.

1. Knowing the disgrace of Jezebel's life and death, why do so many professing Christians show the "spirit of Jezebelism" in their appearance? If the heart were fixed by the Spirit of Christ, why would the face need further fixing (painting, piercing, etc.)? How can a "Jezebel-ish" heart be fixed? Contrast the spirit of Jezebel (1 Kings 9:30, 31) with Sarah's (1 Peter 3:6).

2. Does God see the fads adopted by "redeemed women" today as any less serious than He did the fads of Israelite women several thousand years ago? Compare the items mentioned in Isaiah 3:16-23 with fashions of our day. Does He want to redeem people from the fads of fashion today?

3. Discuss the purposes of clothing: 1) to cover the body adequately - Why? 2) a means of identity, 3) weather protection, 4) to maintain morality and decency. Are there others?

4. The Bible mentions modest apparel for redeemed women. What are some Bible principles concerning the outward appearance of redeemed men?

5. A wolf can dress in sheep's clothing and do his deceptive work. But why do today's saints insist that there's nothing wrong with sheep wearing wolves' clothing? Is that deception one of the wolf's successful strategies against the modern church?

6. Is the wearing of the robe of righteousness by the saints (Revelation 19:8) limited to the marriage supper of the Lamb, or should it "show here" before arriving there? Is it only a "hidden man of

the heart" matter (1 Peter 3:4), or is it also an external symbol here of our robe in heaven?

Questions submitted by
Elmer Schrock
Stuarts Draft, VA

CHAPTER 4

What Does the World Say About Dress?

Dress styles change constantly. People buy clothes, wear them for a while, and soon they are out of style.

The changing styles gradually uncovered parts of women's bodies. Legs were bared in the 1920's . . . the thighs in the 1960's. Today women wear less clothing than in any other period since ancient time. Why? What's behind all this undress?

In the summer of 1997 there was a cold-blooded murder in Miami, Florida that made news headlines around the world. News reporters wrote stories relating to the incident for months following. Not only was it front page news, it was also the subject in the style section and in fashion magazines.

The person who was murdered was a wealthy man. He had a 26,000 square foot home in Miami valued at approximately three million dollars. It had 16 bedrooms, two kitchens and a mosaic-lined swimming pool. He had three other houses elsewhere in the world.

As I read the story of his death, I realized this man was a worldly celebrity. The story of his life, his work, and his wealth shed some light on the world of fashion. It opened the door further in seeing how Satan uses the unredeemed to break down the principles of God's Word. I saw how Satan uses his servants to attack decency and modesty.

This wealthy celebrity was Gianni Versace, an Italian fashion designer. Here are a few statements that were written about him:

"Designer Gianni Versace understood that fashion was about more than clothes. He knew that a simple dress could also make allusions to art, music, architecture, and the cult of celebrity."

"His style was flamboyant, profoundly sexy, and often crossed the line into a wonderful, dangerous vulgarity."

"He unapologetically cut dresses obscenely low or ridiculously high. But he could also cut a perfect suit that blended classic lines with delicate sensuality."

"Fashion for him was a glamorous, colorful, sensual world."

"He was a homosexual and designed men's wear accordingly."

These statements come from the fashion world and its editors. Do they tell you something about the world's approach to attire? How do Versace's principles line up with the Word of God? They don't! They are opposites!

The Bible explains the principles of the world.

"Love not the world, neither the things that are in the world. If any man love the world, the love of the Father is not in him. For all that is in the world, the lust of the flesh, and the lust of the eyes, and the pride of life, is not of the Father, but is of the world. And the world passeth away, and the lust thereof: but he that doeth the will of God abideth for ever" (1 John 2:15-17).

The Bible is clear—you cannot love God and the world. Your heart is with one or the other.

All that is in the world is not from the Father, but from the world.

Lust of the flesh—the craving for sensual gratification.

Lust of the eyes—greedy longings of the mind.

Pride of life—assurance in one's own resources or the stability of earthly things. These are from the world.

Love for money.

"But they that will be rich fall into temptation and a snare, and into many foolish and hurtful lusts, which drown men in destruction and perdition. For the love of money is the root of all evil: which while some coveted after, they have erred from the faith, and pierced themselves through with many sorrows" (1 Timothy 6:9,10).

The love and drive for money is the root of evil. The Bible here says the root of all evil—"all sorts of evil."

Merchants love money! It is their love for money that will cause them to put lewd films in the theaters and video stores and pornography on the market.

The desire for money is also what drives many to merchandise that which is regarded as sexy. *Style* magazine ran an article entitled "what's Sexy Now." This article listed "25 Fashion Rules You Should Know." Two of them were:

"Black is the sexiest color on women."

"Plastic shopping bags lower the 'wow' factor in whatever you're wearing." Because of the lust for profits, merchants will utilize these rules in the market place.

Preachers have told us that the world dresses to reveal. Fashion designers and news reporters have made no bones about this. That's their aim. They operate out of the lust of the flesh, the lust of the eye, and the love of money. Fashion editors and writers explicitly and plainly reveal this in their reporting. My goal is to expose the intent of the fashion industry and the force that propels it. I am somewhat torn between laying it all out as they say it so that you are sure to get the depth of their vanity, and respecting decency itself. Some of the writers' descriptions of Vanity Fair defy decency of the pulpit and Christian literature. However, I want to tell you enough so that by the convicting power of the Holy Spirit you will develop a hatred for the fashions of this world.

The designers and their fashions.

The *World Book Encyclopedia* says, "No one knows exactly why or when people first wore clothes." They "probably began 100,000 years ago. Throughout history, many people have worn clothing more for decoration than covering the body. Most people wear clothing that makes them feel attractive."[1]

The *World Book* is wrong on the first statement. The redeemed believe the Bible tells us when people started to wear clothes. The *World Book* is right on their second statement that people wear clothing for decoration:

"People wear clothing for decorations." That is what fashion designers thrive on. Here is what reporters say about their work:

"He could produce dresses and pants suits that roared with aggression."

"He could craft a skirt that seduced the eye with a flutter of a well placed ruffle."

He was noted for designing "vulgar slits and sleazy slacks," and clothing for both men and women that were considered wild, and would stir the passions.

One designer's line described "this sort of sexy, flat front, old-fashioned cut." "The pants didn't simply look bleached but rather lived-in, scarred, almost dirty."

This designer gave the signal that "it's once again okay, indeed fabulously hip to shuffle about in a pair of beleaguered dungarees."[2]

The designers make use of ruffles, slits, cuts, ribbons, buttons, and the color of buttons to appeal to the "lust of the flesh." Fashion designers are a part of the ungodly world system that fights against the principles of God. The father of the fashion world is the devil. The fruit the fashion designers produce indicates they are propelled by the spirit of the devil.

The *World Book* spoke correctly for the unredeemed: they dress to make themselves look attractive.

The runway.

How do designers get their latest fashions to go into shopping bags with receipts attached? They start by displaying their designs at seasonal fashion shows. Models are hired to wear their latest collections and walk the runway into the audience. Designers bring their favorite models and send them marching across the runway through the crowd that attends.

A few lines from reporters describe the activity:

> "The menswear season was kicked off this morning by Calvin Klein. This week will include designer Alexander Julian stepping back into the spotlight with his signature collection. The Gant line will take to the runway for the first time. . . . John Bartlett is expected to infuse energy into menswear week when he shows his line on Thursday."[3]

> "When stylish women saw super-models teetering down the runways in high-attitude footwear at this season's fashion shows, they tossed aside their comfy shoes for pointy toes and pipe thin heels. . . ." One retailer has a waiting list for the $395.00-a-pair "nail" shoes, named for the 4½ inch sliver of a metal shaft that functions as a heel.

> "For the spring collection they showed this afternoon, they used transparent black metal mesh to create a skirt that falls just above the knee. A modest gray skirt with a peek-a-boo side slit was worn."

> "Two designers . . . created a collection that was sexy, sophisticated and just a little naughty."[4]

> "It was noted that one designer put the super-models on his runway. There was no place for a 'girl' who 'wasn't bursting with attitude, sensuality and the ability to arouse the audience with the sway of the hips.'"[5]

The runway is where the designers show their ware, where celebrities flock for front seats, and clothing is displayed that promotes the sins of Sodom and Gomorrah. It's where the ridiculous is introduced, such as pants so tight one can hardly get them on or so low one cannot walk in comfort. The runway is where designs are promoted that war against the principles of the Bible.

The designers' schemes and the fashion shows are part of the process. Their aim is to connect you with their product at the point where a sales clerk closes the drawer of the cash register, hands you a receipt, and says "thank you for shopping at . . ."

The advertising.

The product is designed and introduced on the runway. Next comes the advertising. That's part of the process to make you want what they have to sell.

An editorial in the *Washington Times* spoke of this issue: "Calvin Klein knows how to sell denim." The designer's advertising concept, "Put nubile young women in tight jeans." Billboards across America proclaimed that "nothing could come between her and her Calvins."

Then comes Mr. Calvin's T.V. ad that is so lewd that a secular editorial called it "all the sickening cliches of New York's child-sex industry."[6] Calvin Klein will push to the bottom, and below, of community-accepted standards to sell his products.

Advertisers go to extremes to sell their product. Here is one that an advertising age magazine critic called "brilliant and wickedly funny."

> "Is it tacky and tasteless—or hip, wry and irreverent? You make the call."

Here's the set up! The T.V. screen fills with grim faces of six pallbearers shouldering a casket down the steps of an old church. With due deliberation they walk to a waiting hearse, wherein they place their burden. The black and white images are stark and grainy.

You might think it's a public service announcement warning about the consequences of drug abuse or gun violence. Nope. It's a commercial for *Britches Great Outdoors*, the sportswear retailer based in Herndon.

The "punch line" of the ad comes in the final few seconds, via voice-over: "You're going to be wearing a suit for a loooong time. Dress comfortably . . . while you can."[7]

What's the point of this T.V. ad? It was run to catch the attention of men aged 18 to 34. The purpose of the ad? Comfort is not their goal as the ad suggests. It is to get men inside their store to leave their money and walk out with a bag of clothes.

Extensive and targeted advertising is one of the methods used to get the public to buy the designer's product. While trying to gather some figures on what Americans spend on fashions and cosmetics, I was told that last year the industry spent 890 million dollars in magazine advertising of cosmetics and toiletries, and one billion 265 million for T.V. commercials.

Some years ago there was a much used ad that said, "We just want to make you happy." That's loaded with deception. What they really want is to make you discontented enough to believe you can buy contentment and happiness. Much of today's advertising runs counter to the Scripture's teaching that the redeemed should be content with food and raiment.

> "But godliness with contentment is great gain. For we brought nothing into this world, and it is certain we can carry nothing out. And having food and raiment let us be therewith content" (1 Timothy 6:6-8).

64

The advertisers are driven by the lust of the eye, the pride of possession, and love for money.

The merchants are ready!

In addition to product advertising the merchants put on the push to get people inside their doors. If they can get you inside, the chances are pretty good they will get some of your money.

Here is a sample from the *Tribune-Review*, a newspaper from the Pittsburgh area, in an article, "Shopsurfing with Popsy." Here are a few quotes from Popsy's column.

> "Fall clothing is arriving today at Personalized Colors . . . in downtown Greensburg and the fabrics are wonderfully exciting! Put this on your shopping list at Personalized Color: colors for fall are rich chocolate birsun, warm olive, bronze, claret, and pine green with some accents of mango and krivie . . . Suede vests are a nice alternative in place of a jacket . . . the flat front skirt and pants, giving a lean look.
>
> Summer clearance continues . . . lots of sizes still available at reduced prices."

Popsy then focuses on a jewelry store in Ligonier that is the place to shop for elegant jewelry at affordable prices. They are having a remodeling sale where you can save up to 60% on earrings and gold chains imported from Italy.

She spiced the article with a quotation, "Most salesmen try to take the horse to water and make him drink. Your job is to make him thirsty."[8]

You might say to yourself, I shop at my favorite Mart where they don't focus on fashions. The Mart I visited last week had signs throughout their clothing department: "Style matters," "Style and Quality," "Great styles for the kids." "Always low prices on all your fashion needs." Here is part of the deception. People do not have *fashion needs*; they have fashion wants. The merchants appeal to the lust of the eye.

Here is another sample:

> "Welcome—the latest styles. Try this: Go check out one of those expensive 'trendy' stores, then go to Target. Anything look familiar? At Target we have trendspotters who travel the world to bring you the latest in everything from fashion to housewares. (Ours cost less, too!)"

I've been looking for a decent, solid-color, zipper jacket with two pockets on the outside and couldn't find any at the Mart stores. Why? The fashion designers haven't told us that is what we need, and the models haven't worn them recently on the runway for the "trendspotters" to go back and tell the merchants this is what will sell.

The influence!

Do the designers, the models, the advertisers, and the merchants have an influence on people? Does it work? Of course it does. I was told that Americans spend three billion, 450 million dollars per year for men's accessories. That includes neckties, gloves, etc. Ties and gloves are not considered clothing—but accessories. The expenditures for women was more, 3 billion, 552 million. Combined, over 7 billion dollars is spent annually in America for accessories.

> "Fashion forecast: 'It's hip to be prep.'"
> "Buffy is determined not to look like the sweet little school girl her conservative mother wants her to be, so she has come up with a few fashion reforms.

"She doesn't tuck in her long sleeved t-shirt. The shrunken look is really in . . . but Buffy doesn't go so far as to let her bellybutton show; she'll save that for the weekend. Her shoes are new—brown, lace-up, big soled boots."[9]

The Fall Fashion Issue of *The Washington Post Magazine* drew attention to "what's cool for kids." In this issue they said, "We step into the eternal, heated debate between kids and parents over the line between outrageously cool and just outrageous." The magazine pictured clothes that were supposed to be "cool for kids." Below the pictures were responses from the teenagers and their moms. Sample responses: Teenager said, "Interesting", Mom said, "yuck." The price of the thing—$44.00. Price of the suede shoes, $355.00.

The baggy pants, the tiny top, with part of the body showing, "Trash" said one mother. "It's the look that a lot of teenagers are going for," said the 15-year-old.[10] The influence of the fashion world keeps this conflict between parents and teenagers alive and ongoing.

The influence reaches beyond the home. *The Sarasota Herald* had a "yuckie" picture on the front page of its January 12, 1998, metro issue. It was a close-up of a tongue extended out of the mouth with a stainless steel "barbell" attached. Police departments are confronted with what to do about body piercing in the ranks. May a police officer wear jewelry in a pierced tongue?

Some call it hip—others call it sick. A 27-year-old deputy said, "I call it self expression, but some people call it sick."

Fashion and fad backed by aggressive advertising

is a powerful influence in our society. It is a continuous conflict in the home, the school, the workplace, and unfortunately, in the church. It is a continuous debate in churches who attempt to be true to the Scriptures.

The reason!

What's the reason for the merry-go-round of spring and fall fashions? Why wide ties—then narrow—then wide? Why tight pants—then baggy? Why the hemline up and down—back up and back down? It's to get your money!

Calvin Klein understands these dynamics. He has built a fortune by linking sex to commerce. By appealing to the lust of the flesh and eye, they are able to influence the people to put much of their money at the altar of the Calvin Klein fashion industry.

Money and greed is what the fashion circuses are about. Imagine people paying $950.00 for a jacket and $555.00 for a skirt with a slit that exposes the leg. When I was a boy our poor neighbors and friends came by and bought empty feed bags to make clothes. They paid something like 25¢ per bag. In those days feed was sacked in bags that were usable for making clothes. Our neighbor's "feed sack clothes" were more decent than those $550.00 so-called skirts.

In May 1996 there was an article in the *Washington Post* that got my attention. The title, *"In Excess We Trust."*

> The author wrote, "The type of house we buy, the car we drive, the clothes we wear are the most vivid means we have of expression, of identifying ourselves with a

68

particular class or lifestyle or mind set.

"As a result, buying goods becomes powerfully seductive, a task which requires constant attention, constant maintenance. Ties grow wide, then narrow, then settle back in between. Skirts go up, then down, then up again. New models come out every year, of cars, bicycles, stereos, that make what we have seem conspicuously outdated or utterly obsolete. How perfect for capitalism: to teach us to be dissatisfied with what we have."

The article points out a lot of foolish facts about ourselves. Unfortunately, the author had no solutions. The closing line is, "See you at the mall."

We have been taught that what's good for business is good for America. Is that really true? Is there no way of escape? Jesus told us this is what the Gentiles—the heathen—go after. They spend much time, money, and worry over what to wear and what to eat.

You who are redeemed by the blood of Jesus Christ, who presently profess to have the garment of salvation, and who expect to meet God on the day of judgment with a robe of righteousness, can you possibly believe that your Redeemer does not care if you copy from the world of fashion? Professing to have a spotless garment of salvation and at the same time trying to keep up with the fashion world is a disgrace to the Redeemer.

Do we have to "see you at the mall"? Is that the only way? Is there a way of escape for the redeemed? Yes, there is! God's Word commands it, and He empowers those who will to do it.

"I beseech you therefore, brethren, by the mercies of God, that ye present your bodies a living sacrifice, holy, acceptable unto God, which is your reasonable service.

69

And be not conformed to this world: but be ye transformed by the renewing of your mind, that ye may prove what is that good, and acceptable, and perfect, will of God" (Romans 12:1, 2).

Release and freedom come by giving your body to God. It comes by saying "*no*" to the runway fashions and by renewing your mind with the mind of Christ.

You can have total freedom from the bondage of fashion. You can present your body and the closet of your heart to Jesus Christ. You can invite His Spirit to reveal to you what is consistent with God's Word and what brings honor to the Redeemer. Then you can by the will of your heart and the power of the Holy Spirit be liberated from the bondage of fashion.

As the Bible states:

> "Ye are of God, little children, and have overcome them: because greater is he that is in you, than he that is in the world" (1 John 4:4).

Questions for Discussion

[1] *World Book Encyclopedia* No. 4, 1984.
[2] *Washington Post*, July 22, 1997
[3] *Washington Post*, July 22, 1997
[4] *Washington Post*, October 9, 1997
[5] *Washington Post*, July 16, 1997
[6] *Washington Times* editorial, August 29, 1995 "Calvin Klein and Kiddie Porn."
[7] *Washington Post*, October 18, 1994
[8] *Tribune Review*, August 8, 1997
[9] *Metropolitan Times*, August 8, 1995
[10] *Washington Post Magazine*, September 14, 1997

1. What is the purpose for clothing according to the world? According to God's Word?
2. How do the principles of the world and the principles of God's Word differ (1 John 2:15-17)?
3. Why are people susceptible to the wiles of the fashion designers? How do fashion designers ensnare people (1 Timothy 6:6-8)?
4. What motivates the world's fashions (1 John 2:16, 17)?
5. In what ways do the redeemed unwittingly allow the world to influence their clothing (Romans 12:1, 2)?
6. How can the redeemed escape the tenacious grip of the fashion world?

Questions submitted by
Glen Yoder
Middleburg, IN

CHAPTER 5

Four Guiding Freedom Principles

I went to visit my neighbor Sid whose wife had been buried several days earlier in a Jewish cemetery in Pennsylvania. I knocked on the door and was welcomed inside. The moment I stepped in the door I was greeted with a stench that invited retreating. It smelled like his cats used the living room for a litter box. It was really strong. I went to visit Sid to let him know I care. The conversation began and I listened to his sorrow and disappointments. After a while I hardly noticed the terrible stench. I got used to it. It no longer bothered me like it had. Sid lives with it and probably doesn't even know it stinks. That is the way apostasy works. It is the way drifting from God's principles takes place. We neglect the principles and soon we do not think much about it. However, God never gets "used to" neglect of His principles!

The redeemed are the people who have realized their sinful condition before God and have become aware that they were caught in the trap of sin. They realized that their sins were uncovered and openly seen by God. They also realized they needed a redeemer to cover, to take away, to release them from their bondage of sin.

The redeemed are the people who have truly repented of sin and have turned to Jesus Christ the Redeemer. They have confessed His name; they have sought and received His forgiveness. The redeemed are assured of the garment of salvation in this present sinful generation. They also expect to stand before God on the day of judgment with a robe of righteousness that was provided by Jesus Christ and was paid for by His shed blood when He was scourged and crucified. The redeemed are the ones who anticipate being at the marriage supper of the Lamb with new robes, clean and white.

The writer of the beloved hymn, "Rock of Ages," expresses his need of God's grace to cover the shame of sin. Think of the terribleness of sinners standing before God in the shame of their sins. Ponder the deep meaning of the expressions for the need of grace:

"Nothing in my hands I bring,
Simply to thy cross I cling;
Naked come to thee for dress;
Helpless, look to thee for grace;
Foul, I to the fountain fly,
Wash me Saviour, or I die."

The non-redeemed are those who continue to live in their sins and have not put on the garment of salvation. The non-redeemed will stand before God with their sins exposed and without a robe of righteousness. The shame of their sins is not covered by the blood of Jesus Christ. They will be expelled from the presence of God and His saints to live with Satan forever in their sinful condition.

The redeemed will be enjoying the presence of Jesus with their sins covered while the non-redeemed will be haunted and tormented because their sins are uncovered and always before them.

God provided the garment of salvation through the shed blood of Jesus Christ. The putting on and wearing of clothing is a daily reminder of your need for the blood of Christ to cover your sins. It can be a regular reminder of the priceless gift of the garment of salvation that you will have on the day of judgment.

The Scriptures give the redeemed principles to follow that will honor and please the Redeemer. The redeemed Christian who has the garment of salvation and walks in righteousness becomes a "stranger and pilgrim" in this sinful and adulterous world. The redeemed pilgrim passes through an ungodly world that is hostile toward the principles of God's Word. The pilgrim makes the Christian journey through an environment in which Satan constantly opposes and attacks God's standard of attire.

John Bunyan explained why Christian and Faithful were persecuted in Vanity Fair.

> "First, the pilgrims were clothed with such kind of raiment as was diverse from the raiment of any that traded at that Fair. The people, therefore, made a great gazing: some said they were fools . . . bedlams . . . outlandish men.
>
> "Secondly, . . . few could understand what they said; they naturally spoke the language of Canaan, but they that kept the Fair were men of this world, so that they seemed barbarian each to the other.
>
> "Thirdly, . . . these pilgrims set very light by all the wares sold at the Fair; they cared not so much as to look

upon them, but looked upwards, signifying that their trade and traffic was in heaven."[1]

Bunyan's expression of the battle with Vanity Fair over 300 years ago is still relevant today. The Christian and Faithful who sojourn in America are faced with the constant pressure of the money-hungry fashion world. The constantly changing fashion industry, Vanity Fair, appeals to the lust of the flesh to stir the ego to glorify itself with appealing apparel. The industry spends billions of dollars to get people hooked on fashion. The media gives it attention, and most major newspapers have a fashion section and editor.

Bunyan said of Christian and Faithful, "These pilgrims set very light by all the wares sold at Vanity Fair; they cared not so much as to look at them."

Oh, if only that were still true today! Vanity Fair has crossed over and won the heart of the so-called church. Most churches in America show a rich representation of Vanity Fair. They have bought into the system and given their money to the god of fashion. When the congregations gather for their Sunday morning service, the music becomes loud and the voices say, "I will sing of my Redeemer" as they emotionally express themselves with singing words, but the items and wares from Vanity Fair dangle on their bodies. Is God pleased with this mixture of religion and fashion? I understand from Scripture that it is an abomination to Him. While the church people may have gotten used to the stench, God has not!

The Christian is called to live in freedom from the pressures of the world. The redeemed can be set free from this fashion bondage. They are to walk in humility and modesty and be a light to those walking in darkness and under the bondage of Vanity Fair.

I will draw attention to four principles of Scripture. If you willingly and carefully follow these, you can enjoy the freedom of being released from the urge to glorify yourself or impress others with your clothing. These Scriptures apply to all of life, including the attire of the redeemed.

Principle #1. Love God intimately.

God wants a close, loving relationship with you. He wants you to love Him with all your heart.

> "But when the Pharisees had heard that he had put the Sadducees to silence, they were gathered together. Then one of them, which was a lawyer, asked him a question, tempting him, and saying, Master, which is the great commandment in the law? Jesus said unto him, Thou shalt love the Lord thy God with all thy heart, and with all thy soul, and with all thy mind. This is the first and great commandment. And the second is like unto it, Thou shalt love thy neighbour as thyself. On these two commandments hang all the law and the prophets" (Matthew 22:34-40).

Jerry thinks he loves Marjorie. He wants to have a closer relationship with her. So he sets out to learn what pleases her. He discovers that she likes chocolate ice cream, light blue is her favorite color, and she enjoys biking.

Ah—Jerry goes shopping. Light blue shirt, pants, socks, shoes, and shoe strings! Then he borrows his uncle's light blue car to take Marjorie to Jerry's Ice Cream shop—then on across town to the bike trail. Does the trail have light blue violets along the way?

And this final question—is there an ice cream shop anywhere close to the trail? Jerry loves Marjorie! Therefore, he wants to do things that please her.

One of the ways you can tell if people love you is that they will try to do what pleases you. One expression of the lack of love is doing what displeases the other person.

Our love for God is expressed in a similar way. If you love God with all your heart, soul, and strength, you will be truly conscious of obeying and pleasing Him. This translates into God being the first and foremost person you want to honor with your clothing. Your question will not be whether it exalts and glorifies you. Instead, you will be careful to honor God by applying His principles in your selection of clothes.

God, I love you! What will honor you most in my attire and appearance? Lord, my heart's desire is to please you and not exalt and glorify myself.

Principle #2. Deny self and take your cross.

"And he said to them all, If any man will come after me, let him deny himself, and take up his cross daily, and follow me. For whosoever will save his life shall lose it: but whosoever will lose his life for my sake, the same shall save it. For what is a man advantaged, if he gain the whole world, and lose himself, or be cast away? For whosoever shall be ashamed of me and my words, of him shall the Son of man be ashamed, when he shall come in his own glory, and in his Father's, and of the holy angels" (Luke 9:23-26).

"If a person wills to come after Jesus, let him deny himself, that is, disown himself, forget, lose sight of himself and his own interests, refuse and give up himself— and take up his cross daily, and follow Me [that is, cleave steadfastly to me, conform wholly to my example, in living and if need be in dying also]" (Luke 14:27, Amplified).

Here is clear, strong language on cross-bearing. If you do not take up your cross and follow Jesus, you cannot be His disciple.

Jesus Christ took up His cross and carried it toward Calvary. Bearing that cross meant continued mockery from the crowd as Jesus was led toward Golgotha. Just think of it. Jesus Christ, the sinless Son of God, was condemned to die. While the sinful, mocking crowd looked on, "He bearing His cross went forth into a place called in the Hebrew Golgotha" (John 19:17). We are told that somewhere on the way to Calvary an onlooker named Simon was compelled to carry the cross. Don't let the fact that Simon carried the cross distract from Jesus' bearing His cross all the way to the point of death. Even though Simon literally carried it part of the way, Jesus "bore" it all the way. It was right there with Him. He identified with it, moved along with it with the will to die on it. The cross of Jesus meant death. He took up His cross and died on it for your sins.

If you want to be a disciple of Jesus, you must deny self and take up your cross daily and follow Jesus Christ. Does this mean you should buy a little golden cross on a chain and carry it? As the cross meant death to Jesus Christ, your cross means death to your self-life. It means dying to self-ego, self-glorification, self-exaltation, self-satisfaction, self-decoration and replacing it with full loyalty to Jesus Christ and the Word.

Taking up your cross means doing what pleases Jesus Christ, whether others do it or not.

It means continuing obedience, even if others make fun of you.

Taking up your cross is loyalty to Jesus and the teaching of the Scriptures in persecution and in affluence.

Look at the context of Luke 9:24: "If any man will come after me." Many people hear about the love of Jesus and say, "I'll accept Christ." However, the first step given here is self-denial, that is, a willingness to obey in full and to die for Christ, if that is what it takes. Baptism into Jesus Christ is a baptism unto death. I'm ready to die for obedience to Jesus Christ. I'm laying down my self-made plans for my life and giving Jesus Christ full access to my heart.

The second step in this Scripture is taking up your cross *daily*. This means on an everyday basis you will do what honors Jesus, even if people make fun of you.

Notice verse 24. If you try to salvage your wonderful self with all your abilities and accomplishments, you will lose it all. If you try to gain the whole world, it will all seep through your fingers.

As I write this, America mourns the death of Frank Sinatra. A young man knelt in prayer outside Sinatra's house in Beverly Hills. My friend, if Mr. Sinatra did not deny his self-life, take up his cross, and follow Jesus, he is not a "happy camper" today. No amount of prayer or mourning here on earth can change where "the tree falleth."

You may say, "Simon, this verse says nothing about dress!" This principle and Scripture apply to anything Satan uses to exalt self or make self look good. This principle applies to whatever tactic Satan uses to inflate self. It applies to whatever trick or trinket he employs to reach his goal.

Does this apply to attire or dress? What does it say in relation to what the redeemed wear? It applies to every area of dress that seeks to exalt, satisfy, or promote self.

Remember, the world designs so-called clothing to appeal to the lust of the flesh, the lust of the eyes, and the pride of life. The world (Vanity Fair) constantly shows off its latest designs to lure people to give their money to the gods of fashion.

The world's own handbook affirms that her principles of dress are to exalt self.

It is my conclusion that the call to discipleship includes the call to denounce and deny the world of fashion. The disciple of Jesus Christ is to daily say no to the fashions and constantly changing fads that the fashion industry shows off on the runway. Taking up your cross when "everybody is doing it" means that you say *no* to Vanity Fair and carefully follow the principles laid out in the Word of God.

Principle #3. Don't conform.

"I beseech you therefore, brethren, by the mercies of God, that ye present your bodies a living sacrifice, holy, acceptable unto God, which is your reasonable service. And be not conformed to this world: but be ye transformed by the renewing of your mind, that ye may prove what is that good, and acceptable, and perfect, will of God" (Romans 12:1, 2).

"Do not conform any longer to the pattern of this world, but be transformed by the renewing of your mind.

Then you will be able to test and approve what God's will is—His good, pleasing and perfect will" (Romans 12:2, NIV).

"Do not be . . . adapted to its external, superficial customs" (Amplified).

There are three things to do in order to know the will of God.

1. Present your bodies a living sacrifice to God. A sacrifice is something you give and surrender. It means offering yourself—your life—your inner-most desires to God. It means a decisive dedication of your body to God. God, I want the deeds of my body to worship you.

2. Do not conform to the pattern of the world. This means making a heartfelt, sincere decision to say *no* to the world of fashion. For conservative Anabaptist believers it means being true to the baptismal vow of renouncing the world and the works of darkness. There is no doubt in my mind that to "be not conformed to this world" does include the world of fashion. As the Amplified says, "Do not be conformed to the external superficial customs." To experience true deliverance from the fashion rat race, say *no* to it. Ask the Holy Spirit to develop a hatred in your heart toward its bondage.

3. Receive a renewed mind. This means putting on the mind of Christ. It means: "Lord Jesus, give me the same attitude and mind about the fashion and fads of the present world as You have." It means agreeing with God's Word to "Love not the world, neither the things that are in the world. If any man love the world, the love of the Father is not in him" (1 John 2:15).

Isn't it shocking that a church which had once pro-claimed a disciplined dress code can drop it and in a few quickly passing years change her dress to fit right into the culture? Instead of not gazing on Vanity Fair, they now embrace it. Isn't it shocking that in a few more years the same church is in confusion and disar-ray on issues like divorce, remarriage, and homosexual behavior? No, I'm not really shocked. That strengthens my faith in the Word of God.

As I gathered information on how the world approaches dress, my eyes were opened to the truth of Scripture. If you want to know the will of God, you cannot be conformed to the world. Any person who follows after and complies to the fashions and fads that come off the world's runway is clouding his ability to see the will of God.

> Follow the Scripture teaching that says, "Come out from among them, and be ye separate, saith the Lord, and touch not the unclean thing; and I will receive you" (2 Corinthians 6:17).

Principle #4. For God's glory.

> "Whether therefore ye eat, or drink, or whatsoever ye do, do all for the glory of God. Give none offence, nei-ther to the Jews, nor to the Gentiles, nor to the church of God: even as I please all men in all things, not seeking mine own profit, but the profit of many, that they may be saved" (1 Corinthians 10:31-33).

This Scripture takes it all in—whatever you do, do all for the glory of God. "Do all for the glory and honor of God" (Amplified).

The redeemed are graced with the garment of sal-vation and the robe of righteousness. In light of this indescribable gift, how can you respond in relation to clothing? When selecting or making clothing, practice asking yourself—will this honor God? When you are at the store looking at a garment, ask—will this honor God? Will this be an offense to anyone? Am I seeking to please myself, or will I seek "the profit of many, that they might be saved"?

Purchase and make clothing for God's honor and glory and to be of non-offense to others.

Recapping the four principles of Scripture.

1. Love God intimately.
2. Deny self and take your cross.
3. Don't conform.
4. For God's glory.

[1] *Encyclopedia of 7700 Illustrations* #5360.

Questions for Discussion

1. Why were Christian and Faithful persecuted in Vanity Fair?
2. Do today's "Christians" and "Faithfuls" still feel and respond the same way to today's "Vanity Fair"? Explain.
3. The Four Guiding Freedom Principles are:
   A.
   B.
   C.
   D.
4. How is our love for God expressed?
5. What is the result of being embarrassed to identify with the children of God (Luke 9:26)?
6. Why does conformity to the world make it virtually impossible to know the will of God?
7. What areas of our life do the two principles of 1 Corinthians 10:31, 32 affect?

Questions submitted by
Nathan Yoder
Free Union, VA

CHAPTER 6

The High Price of a Beautiful Coat

Do you remember the "bird story" in the first chapter? It was about the preacher who met a boy in front of the church carrying a rusty cage with two little birds inside. The boy was going to play with the birds and then maybe feed them to an old cat they had around the house. The preacher bought the birds and let them fly. Do you remember that the preacher said it seemed the birds were singing "redeemed, redeemed redeemed" as they flew into the blue?

The story of redemption begins in the Bible with two people who were caught and trapped in the cage of sin. Because they committed sin, they lost their godly glory. They were naked and ashamed before God and had no song to sing. The only hope of a song to sing was a promise from God that a redeemer would come and release them from the consequences of their sin. Adam and Eve were driven from their paradise with the assurance from God that an offspring from the woman would *"bruise and tread underfoot"* the head of Satan. (See Genesis 3:15, Amplified.)

Many years later God came to a man named Abram, later called Abraham (scholars believe it may have been around 1700 years later). He called Abram and blessed him with a promise of Christ, the Redeemer, and assured him that *"in thee* shall all families of the earth be blessed"* (Genesis 12:3).

Years later, God spoke to Abram again. This time He told Abram to lift up his eyes and look around. Look north and south, east and west; all the land you see I will give to you and your descendants. "And I will make thy seed as the dust of the earth, so that if a man can number the dust of the earth, then shall thy seed also be numbered" (Genesis 13:16). Later God told Abraham, "I will give unto thee, and to thy seed after thee, the land wherein thou art a stranger, all the land of Canaan, for an everlasting possession" (Genesis 16:8).

God promised the land of Canaan to Abraham's descendants, later known as the Children of Israel. The road to taking possession of their promised land was a long and hard one. The Lord promised Israel that if they obeyed Him diligently, He would fight their battles and drive the heathen nations out of the land. Israel spent many years in slavery in Egypt. Then God sent Moses to bring them out of Egypt into a good land flowing with milk and honey, a land of plenty. After forty years of wandering in the desert, Joshua led them across the Jordan into the land of Canaan. Soon after they crossed the Jordan, God instructed Joshua how to take the city of Jericho.

The Lord told Joshua, "Look, I have given you Jericho. March around the city with your army one time every day for six days. Seven priests shall carry trumpets and march in front of the Covenant Box. On the seventh day march around the city seven times. The priests shall blow their trumpets as they march. Then they are to sound one long blast and all the people will give a loud shout. The city walls will fall and the people will march right into the city."

Joshua ordered the people into action. He got up early in the morning and got the march going. They marched around the city six times just as the Lord had instructed Joshua. On day seven they got up at daybreak and marched around the city. This day they did the march seven times.

Joshua gave them further orders. He instructed the men when to shout. He told them, "The Lord has given you the city." Then he gave more instructions. "The city and everything in it shall be destroyed as an offering to the Lord. Save Rahab as we promised, but do not to take the accursed things in the city." He also reminded them that the silver and gold and things made of bronze and iron belonged to the Lord and were to be set apart for Him. These items were to be put into the Lord's treasury.

Joshua warned the people, "If you take anything for yourselves that was to be destroyed, you will bring trouble and destruction to Israel. If you take of the 'accursed thing,' you will make 'Israel a curse and trouble it'" (Joshua 6:18).

Then the trumpet blew the long blast, the men gave the loud shout, and just as the Lord had said, the walls collapsed. The Israelites went right into the city and captured it. They defeated the city and destroyed it.

This was a giant step toward claiming their promised land. The Lord gave them a miraculous victory. For Israel, this was an easy win! That is what He had promised them if they obeyed Him.

With such an outstanding victory behind them, Israel was ready to press on in possessing the land promised to them by God. Ai was their next move. Joshua sent some men to check out the area. The men came back and reported that there were only a few men in Ai to fight against them. Winning this battle should not have been a problem.

They didn't need a big army to defeat Ai. So they went against Ai with only 3000 men. Instead of a big win, it was a big surprise and miraculous defeat. What happened?

"But the children of Israel committed a trespass in the accursed thing: for Achan, the son of Carmi, the son of Zabdi, the son of Zerah, of the tribe of Judah, took of the accursed thing: and the anger of the LORD was kindled against the children of Israel. And Joshua sent men from Jericho to Ai, which is beside Bethaven, on the east side of Bethel, and spake unto them, saying, Go up and view the country. And the men went up and viewed Ai. And they returned to Joshua, and said unto him, Let not all the people go up; but let about two or three thousand men go up and smite Ai; and make not all the people to labour thither; for they are but few. So there went up thither of the people about three thousand men: and they fled before the men of Ai. And the men of Ai smote of them about thirty and six men: for they chased them from before the gate even unto Shebarim, and smote them in the going down: wherefore the hearts of the people melted, and became as water. And Joshua rent his clothes, and fell to the earth upon his face before the ark of the LORD until eventide, he and the elders of Israel, and put dust upon their heads. And Joshua said, Alas, O Lord GOD, wherefore hast thou at all brought this people over Jordan, to deliver us into the hands of the Amorites, to destroy us? would to God we had been content, and dwelt on the other side Jordan! O Lord, what shall I say, when Israel turneth their backs before their enemies! For the Canaanites and all the inhabitants of the land shall hear of it, and shall environ us round, and cut off our name from the earth: and what wilt thou do unto thy great name? And the LORD said unto Joshua, Get thee up; wherefore liest thou thus upon thy face? Israel hath sinned, and they have also transgressed my covenant which I commanded them: for they have even taken of the accursed thing, and have also stolen, and dissembled also, and they have put it even among their own stuff. Therefore the children of Israel could not stand before their enemies, but turned their backs before their enemies, because they were accursed: neither will I be with you any more, except ye destroy the accursed from among you. Up, sanctify the people, and say, Sanctify yourselves against tomorrow: for thus saith the LORD God of Israel, There is an accursed thing in the midst of thee, O Israel: thou canst not stand before thine enemies, until ye take away the accursed thing from among you. In the morning therefore ye shall be brought according to your tribes: and it shall be, that the tribe which the LORD taketh shall come according to the families thereof; and the family which the LORD shall take shall come by households; and the household which the LORD shall take shall come man by man. And it shall be, that he that is taken with the accursed thing shall be burnt with fire, he and all that he hath: because he hath transgressed the covenant of the LORD, and because he hath brought folly in Israel. So Joshua rose up early in the morning, and brought Israel by their tribes; and the tribe of Judah was taken: and he brought the family of Judah; and he took the family of the Zarhites: and he brought the family of the Zarhites man by man; and Zabdi was taken: and he brought his household man by man; and Achan the son of

Carmi, the son of Zabdi, the son of Zerah, of the tribe of Judah, was taken. And Joshua said unto Achan, My son, give, I pray thee, glory to the LORD God of Israel, and make confession unto him; and tell me now what thou hast done; hide it not from me. And Achan answered Joshua, and said, Indeed I have sinned against the LORD God of Israel, and thus and thus have I done: when I saw among the spoils a goodly Babylonish garment, and two hundred shekels of silver, and a wedge of gold of fifty shekels weight, then I coveted them, and took them; and, behold, they are hid in the earth in the midst of my tent, and the silver under it. So Joshua sent messengers, and they ran unto the tent; and, behold, it was hid in his tent, and the silver under it. And they took them out of the midst of the tent, and brought them unto Joshua, and unto all the children of Israel, and laid them out before the LORD. And Joshua, and all Israel with him, took Achan the son of Zerah, and the silver, and the garment, and the wedge of gold, and his sons, and his daughters, and his oxen, and his asses, and his sheep, and his tent, and all that he had: and they brought them unto the valley of Achor. And Joshua said, Why hast thou troubled us? the LORD shall trouble thee this day. And Israel stoned him with stones, and burned them with fire, after they had stoned them with stones. And they raised over him a great heap of stones unto this day. So the LORD turned from the fierceness of his anger. Wherefore the name of that place was called, The valley of Achor, unto this day" (Joshua 7).

Remember that God told Israel repeatedly that if they obeyed His commands, He would bless them, He would make them successful. If they did not obey, they would be without His blessing and instead would experience curse or defeat. Israel was solemnly warned that if they take anything that belongs to the Lord or that should be destroyed, it would mean trouble for all of Israel.

The people did not obey. One person kept some of the things that were to be given to the Lord and that were to be destroyed. The disobedience of one person brought trouble and shameful defeat. It should have been an easy win. God withdrew His blessing just as He promised.

Joshua fell on his face before the Lord till evening. He asked God, "Why did you bring us over here to let the Amorites destroy us? The Canaanites and the other people in the country will hear about this. They will then surround us and kill us. What will that do to Your great *name?"*

The Lord explained to Joshua that it wasn't the Lord. It was Israel. Israel sinned and that sin brought defeat. The commandments of God were broken. That is why the Israelites could not stand before the enemy. What commandments of God were broken? Was it for rape or gross immorality that they were defeated? No, it wasn't such a big thing. Only about five pounds of silver, a pound and a quarter of gold, and a beautiful coat from Babylon. But it was disobedience, and that is serious before the Lord.

God told Joshua He would cease to be with them unless they destroyed the accursed thing. They could not stand before the enemy until the accursed thing was taken away.

What's so bad about taking a little hunk of gold, a little silver, and a beautiful foreign garment?

The gold and silver were to be dedicated to the Lord. That belonged to God. They were to go into the treasury of the Lord. Achan's eyes lusted after them, so he took them and hid them in his tent. The silver and gold were *stolen* from God. The Lord is displeased when His people keep for themselves that which belongs to Him. God's storehouse of blessings ceases to flow out to those who rob God.

Achan's eyes also lusted after the attractive garment he came across in Jericho. "It was an ample robe, probably made of the skin or fur of an animal, and ornamented with embroidery, or perhaps a variegated garment with figures inwoven in the fashion for which the Babylonians were celebrated" (Smith's Bible Dictionary).

Ah—this was a coat that was beautiful to the eyes. Achan said, "When I saw among the spoils a goodly (beautiful), Babylonish garment, . . . I coveted" (Joshua 7:21). This garment caught the lust of his eyes. He longed to have it. Even though it was forbidden, he took it.

It was an expensive take! It cost him his life. Achan's sin caused many of his fellow Israelites to lose their lives in the lost battle. In return, God required his life, the life of his family, and his livestock. And he didn't get to wear his fancy coat in front of his fellow Israelites or use his precious metals to pamper himself. Everything that belonged to Achan had to be destroyed.

God gave a very strong message. He promised His presence if they obeyed. This message says sin has drastic consequences, and God's people should take drastic measures to obey Him.

Most believers would agree that the defeat came because of disobedience. It is noteworthy that part of the deliberate disobedience had to do with clothing.

Achan took a forbidden garment that was to be destroyed. What did that hurt if, after all, it was just a garment?

First, it was a coat from Babylonia that reflected the heathen culture. It blended with the "mainstream" lifestyle of the Babylonians.

Second, the coat was not the distinctive garment for God's people. It did not have the tassels with the blue thread to constantly remind them to obey God's commands. Since God gave Moses specific instructions what the Children of Israel should wear, this foreign garment was a violation of the command.

> "And the LORD spake unto Moses, saying, Speak unto the children of Israel, and bid them that they make them fringes in the borders of their garments throughout their generations, and that they put upon the fringe of the borders a ribband of blue: and it shall be unto you for a fringe, that ye may look upon it, and remember all the commandments of the LORD, and do them; and that ye seek not after your own heart and your own eyes, after which ye use to go a whoring: that ye may remember, and do all my commandments, and be holy unto your God. I am the LORD your God, which brought you out of the land of Egypt, to be your God: I am the LORD your God (Numbers 15:37-41).

Third, the "beautiful coat" appealed to the lust of the eye. It glorified the selfish ego rather than showing a love for God. When Achan saw the coat, he very much wanted it for himself.

This forbidden coat had defeat factors woven throughout. Coveting and taking it contributed to Israel's degrading defeat. It was a great hindrance in conquering and possessing their promised land.

Is there a lesson to be learned from the Achan experience for the church today (see 1 Corinthians 10:11)? Does clothing have anything to do with the church experiencing spiritual victory or defeat? Does wrong clothing take away the church's witness and power to live above sin?

The Scripture's unchanging instruction for attire of the redeemed is modesty, humility, and meekness that frames the inner beauty of godliness. Attempting to beautify the outward body with "fancy hair, gold jewelry, or fine clothes" is forbidden (1 Peter 3:3, NCV). "They should not use fancy braided hair or gold or pearls or expensive clothes to make themselves beautiful" (1 Timothy, 2:9, NCV). The redeemed focus on being spiritually beautiful in the eyes of God.

The world's ever-changing approach is the opposite. It focuses on making the body the eye catching object. The principles of the world are the lust of the flesh, the lust of the eyes, the pride of life, and the greed for money. It constantly displays its sensual designs on the fashion runway.

Can the church, the redeemed who have the robe of righteousness, copy the patterns and fads from the fashion runway and still be victorious? Can they wear the Babylonish garments and keep their power over the enemy? My understanding of Scripture is—no, they cannot.

Power doesn't mean having the biggest church or largest membership. Power is not a mouth profession and living like the world. Power is the strength to buck the popular tide and do what pleases God.

Remember, Jesus indicted the ministers of the Thyatira church for tolerating Jezebel and allowing her teachings to lead His servants astray.

Remember Isaiah's warning of judgment on the proud and haughty women who contributed to the fall of Judah with their outward vanity?

Remember Zephaniah's warning of God's wrath that would sweep away everything in the land and punish all those in foreign garments?

Israel was promised a land flowing with milk and honey. As Israel was promised a land, so the redeemed have the promise of "a city that hath foundations, whose builder and maker is God" (Hebrews 11:10).

> Jesus said, "In my Father's house are many mansions: if it were not so, I would have told you. I go to prepare a place for you. And if I go and prepare a place for you, I will come again and receive you unto myself; that where I am, there ye may be also" (John 14:2-3).
>
> The redeemed are those who "confessed that they were strangers and pilgrims on the earth" (Hebrews 11:13), and who "desire a better country which is an heavenly: wherefore God is not ashamed to be called their God: for he hath prepared for them a city" (Hebrews 12:16). "For here we have no continuing city, but we seek one to come" (Hebrews 13:14).

The redeemed are the church of Jesus Christ who are making their journey through this world. This is expressed in the songs they sing:

> "This world is not my home, I'm just a passing through. My treasures are laid up somewhere beyond the blue."
>
> "The burdens of life may be many, the frowns of the world may be cold. To me it will matter but little, when I walk up the streets of gold."

"Earth holds no treasures but perish with using.
However precious they be: yet there's a country to which
I am going. Heaven holds all to me."

Can the redeemed who sing the songs of heaven take the Babylonish garments of their day and not reap eventual trouble and spiritual decline? Does attire have anything to do with the church experiencing spiritual victory or defeat? History can give us some helpful insights on the question. With these questions in mind I briefly refer to several church bodies who had once stressed the importance of rejecting worldly attire and keeping the commandments of God.

John Wesley, considered to be the founder of the Methodist Church, preached on the subject of dress. He declared that the Romans 12:1, 2 passage applied "to the apparel of Christians." There was the common idea in the religious world that "there ought to be no difference at all in the apparel of Christians." He regarded that to be a "mistake." He declared that "no book of God" teaches such a thing.[1]

He preached that the wearing of gay or costly apparel:

"tends to breed and increase vanity."

"tends to beget anger . . . and uneasy passion."

"tends to create and inflame lust," and it is directly opposite of being adorned with good works.

In his dying days, Wesley said, "I am distressed." He regretted that he did not do like the Moravian and Quaker brethren and declare, "This is our manner of dress, which we know is both Scriptural and rational."

Where are the Methodists today? Are they known for their loyalty to Scripture and winning spiritual battles for Jesus? On the morning I was researching Wesley's sermon on attire, the *Washington Times* had an article entitled, "Four Faiths Tussle Over Gay Issues." The third paragraph draws attention to the United Methodists' tussle. The "tussle" in this body is over one of their ministers who conducted a marriage of two lesbians. In a recent ecclesiastical church trial the minister was found not guilty of breaking church rules. This is followed by the Council of Bishops assuring the people that the rules barring ordination of homosexuals still stand.

Another article in the same paper was about Methodists in Britain considering selling liquor at conferences and receptions to help raise $13.1 million for a renovation project opposite Westminster Abbey.

The Church of the Brethren was once known for its "order of oneness" in relation to dress and other distinctive church practices. The "order of oneness" was sharpened to define what was suitable as Christian garb. Time eroded their position, and in the early part of the century the Brethren made what is referred to as a watershed dress decision: "Plainness no longer a test of membership." In 1920 they decided, "The necktie should not be a test of membership."[2]

Aside from a small minority of its ministers, the church has ceased speaking on what is proper Christian dress and has allowed the world to handle that issue.

Similar points can be made about the Mennonite Church. Strong defining positions on dress prevailed across the church. Special sessions of Conference adopted statements against worldly attire and the wearing of jewelry. In 1944 the Mennonite General Conference resolved "that we request that Bro. Wenger's address on Historic and Biblical Position of the Mennonite Church on Attire be printed in pamphlet form."

Bro. J. C. Wenger's pamphlet expounded on the Scriptural teaching and made a strong case for the church's position on defining what is acceptable. Today a visit to most Mennonite churches would indicate that their members get their cues for attire from the fashion runway instead of the Scriptures and a faithful church of God. Within the church are those who have rejected the former teachings and now make fun of their leaders and practices of the past.

Can the church take its cues from the world's fashion runway and retain its power and clear direction? The churches I made reference to were admonished about the Biblical commands of attire. Eventually they did not see the need of being faithful in those areas. It was seen as a little thing of not much importance. Today these groups are embroiled in controversy over issues that seem very clear in the Word of God. It appears that the power over sin is gone. There seems to be no clear spiritual direction.

> "He that is faithful in that which is least is faithful also in much: and he that is unjust in the least is unjust also in much" (Luke 16:10).

The redeemed cannot take the Babylonish garment without it having some effect on victorious Christian living. It contributes to confusion and trouble. Following fashion's allurements instead of Scriptural principles brings trouble into the camp of the redeemed. It clouds the clear vision of the promised city whose builder and maker is God. Achan's forbidden garment hindered Israel's possession of the promised land. The church's indulgence in the world's garments today does not bring God's blessing. It does bring trouble and confusion and becomes a besetting sin.

The Bible admonishes the redeemed to lay aside anything that would get in the way or be a hindrance on the journey.

> "Wherefore, seeing we also are compassed about with so great a cloud of witnesses, let us lay aside every weight, and the sin which doth so easily beset us, and let us run with patience the race that is set before us, looking unto Jesus the author and finisher of our faith" (Hebrews 12:1, 2a).

Joshua left a good example for today's redeemed children of God. He "rent his clothes and fell to the earth upon his face before the ark of the Lord." In the spirit of Joshua come before the Lord. "Lord, show me anything in my life that hinders victory. Show me any hidden things in my wardrobe that would hinder your blessing in my life."

It is this spirit of willing submission to God's will that brings His blessing on your life.

[1]J.C. Wenger, *Separated Unto God*. Herald Press. Pg. 323-324.
[2]Carol F. Bower, Brethren Society. Johns Hopkins University Press.

Questions for Discussion

1. a. What beautiful coat was "priced too high"?
   b. What wrong desires motivated its "buyer"?
2. Do the New Testament Scriptures mention and define principles of appropriate dress? If so, what are they?
3. What was John Wesley's view of distinctive dress in his early life? In his later life?
4. What were the first steps worldward taken when the Church of the Brethren started to relax their dress requirements?
5. a. What happens to the church which takes its cues from the world in how to dress?
   b. Does this affect its effectiveness in addressing very obvious violations of God's laws, such as marital infidelity and homosexuality?
6. How may fashionable dress be a weight and a besetting sin?

Questions submitted by
Paul Miller
Partridge, KS

CHAPTER 7

Pillow Prophets—Bondage and Freedom

Few of us would argue whether morals, manners, and behavior have declined sharply in the last several decades. School behavior has declined from shooting "spit wads" with rubber bands to murder with guns. Stories of sexual assault, rape, and early teen pregnancy are scattered throughout our newspapers. Respect for sexual purity might well be on the endangered species list. One of the contributing factors to the dangerous moral decline is the loss of decency in dress. Or should I say, the shameless undress? As immodesty increased, sexual crimes and assault followed. The nation and the church are already reaping bitter consequences for its permissiveness in undress. We have taken down the guardrails and now are becoming overwhelmed in gathering up the tragedies.

There are churches that claim to believe and teach the whole Bible. Somehow they manage to overlook the issue of dress. With all the emphasis the world puts on dress, much of the church seems not to notice and just look the other way. The devil and his world troops attack the church on dress and moral issues. Since the church folks don't want to start a "fuss," they step back in retreat. Satan goes from one victory to another. In many churches, the moral decline has moved so far its ministers wouldn't think of a sermon on immodesty.

Cliff Jennings grew up going to a Bible believing church. He has been in church a lot in his 60-year journey of life, and he says he does not remember ever hearing a sermon on dress. That should be an eye-opener as to why such a moral decline is in our culture.

Many "Bible believing" churches resort to preaching only "believe on the Lord Jesus Christ and thou shalt be saved," and ignore some of the moral issues of which the Scriptures call to repentance.

Old Testament history tells us that God called prophets to warn His people. God has given us the Bible. Today His ministers, or prophets, are to proclaim His Word and will. Ministers of the gospel are to sound the warning for God.

The prophets of today carry much responsibility for the deplorable immorality, indecency, and fashion in the church and the world. Preachers from earlier generations sounded clear warnings against following fashion.

> John Wesley warned: "The putting on of costly apparel is exactly opposite of what the apostle terms the hidden man of the heart."[1]
> Charles Finney taught:
> "It is your duty to dress so plainly as to show to the world that you place no reliance on the things of fashion, and set no value at all on them, but despise and neglect them altogether."[2]

"Evangelists such as Dwight L. Moody were quite vocal in their denunciation [of the fads of their time.] . . . in the early 20th century Billy Sunday and many other less influential pulpiteers thundered against the 'jazz age' fashions and the 'flappers.'"[3]

Ira D. Williams wrote:

"Let your dress be a rebuke to fashion and extravagance, and a model worthy of imitation."[4]

J. C. Wenger in his booklet published in 1944, *Christianity and Dress,* made the point that the Anabaptist reformation included "condemnation of conformity to the world in attire."[5]

Things have changed and so has preaching. Today's preachers are giving an opposite message. Some teach that God wants you to be wealthy and have the finest in clothes. Others boast of having been set free from the legalism of dress codes. Others make fun of their ancestors who stood against the fashion world with dress codes.

Modern day prophets claim God doesn't care how you dress. They declare that God looks at the heart, not the outward appearance. If they teach anything about dress, they compare those who follow a standard to the actions of the scribes and Pharisees whom Jesus condemned. They are gifted in pointing out any hypocrisy found in "plain dressers."

These modern day prophets remind me of the false prophets in Ezekiel's time. Ezekiel was sounding the alarm of judgment. The false prophets developed the art of making God's people comfortable.

David Wilkerson called them the "Pillow Prophets." Ezekiel 13 is the very word of Jehovah against preachers and prophets who accommodate people with flesh-pleasing words they said were from the Lord. These words were designed to make God's people comfortable in the face of impending judgment.

In fact, they were not satisfied to prophesy good times ahead from their great houses of ivory and beds of ease—they sought to provide a pillow for every elbow. "Woe to those who apply pillows to all elbows . . ." (Ezekiel 13:18, Spurell).

> "Behold, I am against your pillows, wherewith ye entice souls . . ." (Ezekiel 13:20).[6]
>
> "Thus saith the Lord God; woe unto the foolish prophets that follow their own spirit, and have seen nothing" (Ezekiel 13:3).
>
> "They have seen vanity and lying divination, saying the Lord saith: and the Lord hath not sent them" (Ezekiel 13:6).

Some of the statements made against the redeemed who practice the Biblical principles of dress are not from the Word of God. The Bible doesn't say God doesn't care how you dress. It doesn't say God doesn't look on the outward. In fact, it says God knows how many hairs are on your head. (Head and hair are outward.)

The modern prophets and their churches look the other way and will not speak out against the immodesty and ungodly dress that has become common place. Even though it ignites the fires of immorality and beastly behavior, they defend and participate in the world of fashion. They choose the pillows of ease rather than to disturb the peace.

Probably the closest I've come to experiencing persecution and ridicule for serving Christ was in relation to my dress. I can recall numerous incidents of the past when remarks and comments were not compliments, but meant as sneers.

My father was a conscientious objector to participating in war during WWI. He was required to spend time at the army barracks in Fort Mead, Maryland. He experienced mockery from the army personnel for refusing to exchange his plain clothes for the uniform of the army. Refusing to follow the world of fashion may bring you some ridicule. It may come from the people of the world, and it may come from people of the church. To live God's principles of dress doesn't give you a bed of ease and comfortable pillows.

Are today's Pillow Prophets really speaking God's truth? They and their sympathizers will tell you that God doesn't look on the outward. When the issue of immodesty or fashionable wear is raised, they often quote the last half of 1 Samuel 16:7.

> "For the Lord seeth not as man seeth, for man looketh on the outward appearance, but the Lord looketh on the heart."

This Scripture is often used as a club to quiet the concerned rather than rightly dividing the Word of Truth. To use it to claim that God doesn't care about the outward appearance is the mark of ignorance and a false prophet.

> "While God may look at a man's heart, we mortals have only his words, his deeds, and his appearance for judging what a man believes. It is certainly a critical error to underestimate clothing's ability to verify or deny what we say with our mouth. The Lord did not rebuke Samuel as some contend for 'looking on the outward appear-

ance.' When the prophet has inclined to prefer the oldest son of Jesse as the next king of Israel, he did exactly what most of us would have done. He used the only criticism available to him at the moment—the outward appearance. The Lord merely reminded Samuel that He had complete knowledge of everything—information that the prophet was not yet privileged to have. The text in no way implies that Eliab's 'appearance' was irrelevant or of trivial concern. In fact, when David, God's selection, was summoned he also had a proper consistent outward appearance."[7]

Scripture draws attention to David's outward appearance.

"David had a healthy reddish complexion, and beautiful eyes, and was fine looking. The Lord said [to Samuel] arise, anoint him: this is he" (1 Samuel 16:12, Amplified).

To say that God doesn't care about the outward appearance is a false teaching and a misrepresentation of Scripture. The first act God did after His conversation with sinful Adam and Eve was getting them properly dressed. He Himself made them presentable to live in the outside world.

Freedom versus bondage.

The spirit of the world and the Pillow Prophets promote the idea that God's principles are bondage. When the redeemed, whether individuals or congregations, take a disciplining position on maintaining godly attire, the attack will follow. They are marked as legalistic and under bondage. The redeemed who make a careful effort to walk in obedience to the Scriptures relating to dress are branded as under bondage. The criticism often comes from others who also claim to be redeemed.

Are the redeemed who take a careful disciplining position to follow the Scriptures really under bondage? Who is really under bondage, those who take a more careful position in following God's ways, or those who reject and eliminate such restraints?

Who really has freedom—the person with a fixed standard or the one who allows the fashion runway to influence what they wear? In the name of freedom many who profess having the garment of salvation have chosen to cast off all restraints of attire and have accepted the ways of the culture. They justify dropping dress standards by boasting of their new freedom.

The devil is a liar and the father of lies. The idea that following God's principles and applying them in everyday life is bondage comes from the father of lies. He deceives people into thinking freedom comes from doing what pleases the eyes (lust of the eyes). He deceives church folks into thinking freedom is increased by following whatever they want from the world of fashion.

Don't be deceived! The fashion world, the lust of the flesh, the lust of the eyes, and the pride of life are not of the Father *"but of the world"* (1 John 2:16). Anything that is of the world does not give true inner peace and satisfaction. It is somewhat like a powerful pain killer to a terminally ill patient: it gives a temporary good feeling. The followers of the fashion principle never arrive. Clothing styles and the accessories people wear are constantly changing. They never arrive!

The people who reject a fixed standard and start to buy into the system liberate themselves into bondage. It's the bondage of the ever-changing, never-arriving world. They make their purchase or copy the design from "what's in." Soon it's "out" and the victim is stuck with something that is neither in style nor in the standard of Scripture.

Imagine planning and starting on a trip to Alaska. Imagine getting on a wrong road and driving a circle forever—and never getting there? Imagine traveling for a year and not getting there. That's what happens to those who liberate themselves into the bondage of the world. They are forever changing apparel but never arriving.

> As the Bible says, "While they promise them liberty they themselves are the servants of corruption: for of whom a man is overcome, of the same is he brought into bondage" (2 Peter 2:19).

True freedom does not come from doing what you want, but from humbly submitting to what is right and pleasing to God.

Eli and Naomi Kauffman are part of a conservative congregation that practices a dress code. He was invited to speak at a ladies Bible study at an Army base near their home in Georgia. After the class they stayed for some informal visiting. One of the ladies was intrigued with his wife's plain attire. She asked some questions about it and learned this was her regular way of dress, even during the week. She remarked, "Oh what freedom." This lady recognized her own burden of keeping up with the fashion world. She could identify the freedom of having an unchanging godly way of dress.

Dress is a statement!

The Pillow Prophets try to tell you it doesn't matter how you dress. In spite of what they say, the way you dress is a statement—it is a language. The Bible gives many references to how people were dressed. It refers to being dressed in sackcloth on the one hand and purple and fine linen on the other. These descriptions of dress are a statement made with clothes.

The book of Proverbs says that a person speaks with the eyes and feet and teaches with the fingers.

> "A naughty person, a wicked man, walketh with a froward mouth. He winketh with his eyes, he speaketh with his feet, he teacheth with his fingers" (Proverbs 6:12,13).

While carefully chosen words help us to communicate, there are many other ways of communicating (blowing the horn and finger-pointing is one of those ways).

There is another form of language that communicates quite clearly. It is a silent speech that gives information about yourself. "This universal though silent language is the way we dress."[8]   Clothing reveals whether your heart has sincerely been dedicated to following God's principles or if you are seeking to exalt yourself. The first impression I get of someone is his appearance. Appearance is the first communication a person gives.

> "It is often forgotten that we never have a second chance to make a good first impression. Many psychologists and psychotherapists claim that nearly 90 percent of what people remember of an initial meeting with someone is through nonverbal communication. Body language, such as posture, facial expressions, hair, and clothing are the keys."[9]

"Our first appearance links us extrinsically with what we represent."[10]

Your clothing is a statement. Your clothes speak for you. On the morning of April 20, 1999, two students of Columbine High School in Littleton, Colorado, stormed the school with guns blazing and murder on their minds. Their black trench coats spoke clearly of what was in their hearts. Their dress was a language and a statement.

One of the marks of the redeemed is that they clean up their foul speech. When a person truly experiences redemption, swearing and the like must go. If his communication with words doesn't change, it is logical to question his repentance and redemption.

Since clothing speaks for you and about you, what does it say when one claims redemption but still follows the lust of the flesh and eyes in dress? What does it say when a person cuts and colors his hair in a ridiculous manner and dyes them in unnatural colors? What speaks the loudest—words or appearance? Does such conduct speak of the Redeemer who gives a robe of righteousness, or does it reflect a heart that is not yielded to God?

Your first impression speaks the loudest. This is one of the reasons I am so strongly opposed to the redeemed wearing sports emblems and insignias. It immediately identifies them as fans of the team rather than disciples of the Redeemer. It is a cloud that hinders the light of the Redeemer.

Should the family of the redeemed have standards?
Should the true prophets and the church take a position on dress? The modern Pillow Prophets described by Ezekiel claim the church shouldn't set a standard.

110

"Nowadays when a plea is made for a Biblical standard of dress in our fundamental churches, schools, camps, or homes, many Christians dismiss the appeal as the peevish tirades of an old crank or fuddy-duddy. **Attempts to establish or enforce a biblical standard of dress are often censored or pitied as nothing more than some misguided 'legalism.'** Even more devastating is when this attitude is found in good, dedicated, gifted, and influential preachers and lay leaders. And the fact is that many in our fundamental circles are less than convinced that it matters how a Christian dresses. This growing segment of Fundamentalism is apparently either ignorant or unconcerned (or both) about the implications of ignoring God's Word in the matter of dress. But before we dismiss the subject as 'much ado about nothing,' we should consider the thoughts of a few secular writers on the importance of how we dress. **History seems to indicate that as a nation degenerates, so, also, do the clearly defined distinctions and standards of dress.** This is especially so in the area of gender identity. Fashion expert, Lawrence Langer, once admonished his readers that: 'The history of civilization has many examples of nations which became effeminate and were destroyed by more virile but less civilized races which conquered and overran them. In all such effeminacy, clothing played a leading role. Thus the wisdom of the ages, which is on the side of sex differentiation in clothes, is based on realities of which most of us do not actually become aware in the short experiences of our life span.'"[11]

As I indicated earlier, if you want to stir up a conflict in the church, talk about what is proper attire, and you'll have it.

Should the church speak on the issue? Remember the approach of the fashion runway? Remember the world's approach to the lust of the flesh, the eyes, the pride of life, and greed for money? For the church to ignore this aspect of Satan's strategy is to see the wolf coming and to say, "peace." As Ezekiel warns, you see the danger but do not sound the warning. "His blood will I require at their hand."

We are now reaping bloodshed, sexual assaults and violence because of immodesty. This is because of the Pillow Prophets' refusing to speak out and warn the people. This is the fruit of those who made fun of the legalistic standard setters.

What about setting standards?

The spiritual leaders of the first century did not fear being dogmatic about their standards.

> "And as they went through the cities, they delivered them the decrees for to keep, that were ordained of the apostles and elders which were at Jerusalem. And so were the churches established in the faith, and increased in number daily" (Acts 16:4, 5).

> "What were these 'decrees' delivered by Paul to the Gentile churches? They were judgments concerning Christian conduct adopted by the elders and people of the Jerusalem church in a business meeting described in Acts 15. The meeting had been called to counteract legalism. The resulting resolution clarified the way of salvation and stipulated guidelines for those who are saved by grace.

> "That church meeting and those decrees dealt with an issue that is being very hotly disputed among Bible-believing Christians today. Do Christian leaders have the right to set standards of life for believers? Many say they do not. Some even call standard-setting 'legalism.' A growing number of men are promoting the idea that leaders should teach the Word but leave the application of biblical principles to the Holy Spirit. Yet 'the decrees' of the Jerusalem council prove that standard-setting is legitimate.

"The decrees forbade three practices: (1) eating meat sacrificed to idols; (2) eating bloody meat; and (3) committing fornication.

"'It seemed good to the Holy Ghost, and to us, to lay upon you no greater burden than these necessary things; that ye abstain from meats offered to idols, and from blood, and from things strangled, and from fornication: from which if ye keep yourselves, ye shall do well. Fare ye well' (Acts 15:28, 29).

"These were 'taboos' prescribed for the Gentile churches. For years, strongly biblical churches in America have observed bans on such practices as social dancing, movie-theater attendance, booze drinking and cigarette smoking. Also forbidden have been playing cards, miniskirts, rock music and hippy hair.

"Now the leaders of Christian youth organizations advocate abandoning the 'taboos.' Radio preachers are saying that social drinking, movie-going and sensual music are 'okay' even for dedicated Christians. Now there is such a thing as 'Christian' rock 'n' roll. Old dress standards are ridiculed in many otherwise conservative churches. Fundamentalist leaders are talking as if the churches made a mistake when they preached the old standards of life for believers.

"Legalism is the new 'boogy-man' condemned by almost everyone, and legalism now means standard-setting. Christian schools are abandoning old standards. Preachers are not preaching against certain things anymore. Times are changing in fundamentalist churches, but things are not getting better!

"Actually, the old standards are more defensible today then they have ever been! Hollywood movies are more immoral and anti-Christian than they were when our spiritual fathers condemned them. Dances are more pagan and sensual than ever. Smoking is now almost universally condemned. Alcohol problems are doing more damage today to our homes, on our highways, and in our society, than before. Yet evangelical leaders are becoming strangely apologetic for the traditional ban their churches have had on such things. How strange, when our condemnation of these activities seems more justified today than in the past!

"A kind of Christian relativism is spreading among us. Folks are saying that God speaks to different believers in different ways about issues of right and wrong. 'The Lord hasn't convicted me about the matter. For you, maybe He is saying it is wrong. For me, it is fine, because I'm not convicted about it.'

"Perhaps that reasoning comes from a twisted interpretation of Romans 14:14 or 1 Corinthians 8:8. But in their context, these verses do not teach any kind of relative morality. Romans 14 recognizes that some interpretations of Bible principles are right, and some are wrong. It then deals with how to react to people who are wrong ('weak').

"Paul calls upon those spiritually stronger to be considerate toward those who are weak, but he never implies that there are no absolute standards. Neither does he teach this in 1 Corinthians 8. The book of 1 Corinthians deals at length with the decrees of Acts 15. The 'bottom line' of chapters 8 and 10 is, 'Don't eat meat sacrificed to idols.' In chapter 8, Paul gives the reasoning behind the decree, but his conclusion is a clear-cut 'don't!'

"**The New Testament teaches** that God has a definite point of view in every issue of life, and that it is our duty to seek it out and follow it.

"'For ye were sometimes darkness, but now are ye light in the Lord: walk as children of light . . . proving what is acceptable in the Lord. . . . Wherefore be ye not unwise, but understanding what the will of the Lord is' (Ephesians 5:8, 10, 17).

"The decrees of the Jerusalem council teach us at least four things about standard-setting: (1) that Christian leaders have the right and duty to set standards of life for the less mature; (2) that the setting of standards is not legalism; (3) that biblically-based standards help individuals and churches; and (4) that the underlying principles for such standards are always applicable."[12]

The spiritual leaders of this century should follow the pattern of the first century church leaders rather than the Pillow Prophets Ezekiel prophesied against.

Is it unscriptural for the church to ask the sisters to wear what is referred to as the cape dress? An interesting note from Adam Clarke should help us understand its roots.

> "Adam Clarke, the Methodist commentator, enlightens us further concerning the word *apparel* in 1 Timothy 2:9. In the Greek it is the compound word, *Katastola*. According to Clarke, the *stola* was a Greek dress—a long piece of cloth which hung down to the feet in front and behind, girded with a belt. The *katastola* was an additional piece of cloth which hung down to the waist loosely over the *stola*. Commenting further Clarke says, 'A more modest and becoming dress than the Grecian was never invented; it was, in a great measure, revived in England about the year 1805, and in it simplicity, decency and elegance were united; but it soon gave place to another mode, in which flippery and nonsense once more prevailed. It was too rational to last long, and too much like religious simplicity to be suffered in a land of shadows, and a world of painted outsides . . . Nothing was ever more becoming than the Grecian *stola*, *katastola*, and belt.' The additional piece of cloth, continuing and known as the *cape* today, serves to more adequately conceal the contour of the body which corrupt women desire to display."[13]

Should the church set a standard? A church that sets no standard on such a daily talked about subject is being irresponsible and negligent by avoiding it.

This appeal to the redeemed!

Remember, the redeemed are the people who have their sins covered by the garment of salvation. They are the ones who, when they meet Christ on the day of judgment, will not meet Him spiritually naked with their sins exposed. They will meet Christ with the scars of sins under the robe of righteousness given to them by Jesus Christ. To preserve God's principles and stand against the principles of the world, I make these six appeals to the redeemed.

1. Be humbly open before God on this matter.

Be assured God cares. Then *will* in your heart for the Holy Spirit to be in complete control. Invite the Holy Spirit into the wardrobe of your heart and the closet of your clothes. Invite God's Spirit to inspect your attire. When you do that, be aware that God often speaks through parents and church leaders.

> "Neither yield ye your members as instruments of unrighteousness unto sin: but yield yourselves unto God, as those that are alive from the dead, and your members as instruments of righteousness unto God. . . . Know ye not, that to whom ye yield yourselves servants to obey, his servants ye are to whom ye obey; whether of sin unto death, or of obedience unto righteousness?" (Romans 6:13, 16).

2. Prayerfully discern who is calling.

When Satan came to Jesus and tempted Him with three approaches, he didn't ask Jesus to do anything that was wrong in itself. Satan asked Him to do good things: perform a miracle of making bread, do a miracle to prove who He is, and gain possession of all the kingdoms of the earth. These were crucially wrong at that time because of who asked Jesus to do them and who would get the honor. I appeal to the redeemed to discern and understand that some things do not belong with the garment of salvation because of who introduced them. If it is from the world's runway, it is likely

116

to disgrace the principles of God. Learn to discern and gladly and willingly say no.

3. Support the church in tackling the issue and seeking a decree. Earlier reference was made to Acts 16 where the first century church made decrees and delivered them to the church "for to keep" (Acts 16:4).

The book of 1 Corinthians deals at length with the *decrees* of Acts 15. The bottom line of chapters 8 and 10 is, "Don't eat meat sacrificed to idols." In Chapter 8 Paul gives the reasoning behind the decree, but his conclusion is a clear cut *"Don't!"* He gives this warning: "But when ye so sin against the brethren and wound their weak conscience, ye sin against Christ" (1 Corinthians 8:12).

The New Testament teaches that God has a definite point of view on every issue of life and that it is our duty to seek it out and follow it.

> "For ye were sometimes darkness, but now are ye light in the Lord: walk as children of light: (for the fruit of the Spirit is in all goodness and righteousness and truth;) proving what is acceptable unto the Lord. . . . Wherefore be ye not unwise, but understanding what the will of the Lord is" (Ephesians 5:8-10, 17).

The decrees of the Jerusalem Council teach us at least four things about setting standards.

a. Christian leaders should set standards.

b. Standard setting is not legalism.

c. Biblically based standards help individuals and churches.

d. The underlying principles are always applicable. Give your support to leaders who are willing to set a standard rather than to be "pillow prophets."

"Be supportive in providing a standard that frees the people from the world system."

4. Lovingly obey the church and leaders.

Lovingly and humbly give your obedience to the churches and leaders who are willing to take a position.

> "A new convert spent some time talking with his pastor about his smoking habit. Yet he could not understand the preacher's teaching about the effects of smoking on his testimony, or about his body and the Holy Spirit.
>
> "Finally, the pastor showed him Hebrews 13:17 and said something like this: 'Bill, right now you are not willing to give up smoking because you do not accept the principles we studied earlier, but could you accept this principle? The Bible says that we should obey our spiritual leaders. You are not mature enough to see why smoking is harmful and wrong for a Christian, but I have had time to grow more than you have, and I know it is wrong. Will you trust me, and just quit smoking because I've told you to do it?'
>
> "The wise young Christian took the preacher up on this proposal and quit his bad habit in compliance with his pastor's 'decree.'"[14]

One of the frustrations of the ministry has been the constant challenge of disobedience and pushing the line of the standards. This is not only frustrating for the ministry, but it takes away the freedom aspect. The one thing you can do to preserve God's principles is to willingly obey where there are set standards.

5. Brothers, dress to complement the sisters.

One of the frustrations of the sisters is that they "stand out," while the brothers can blend right into the crowd. Please, brothers, dress in a manner that will complement the modesty and decency expected from the sisters.

6. Follow the things that speak for Christ and the church.

There is a story about a Civil War soldier who thought he would wear both gray and blue. He reasoned that if he wore the coat of one side and the trousers of the other, neither would shoot at him. It didn't work. Instead of avoiding becoming a target, he was fired upon by both sides. There was no clear identification as to which side he was on.

Follow the biblical principles that clearly identify you as on the side of Christ and the Church.

Think of this: on the day of judgment the redeemed will appear before Christ the Saviour clothed with a "robe of righteousness." They are dressed in the "garment of salvation" awaiting the arrival of their King of kings.

If you are one of the redeemed, should not your earthly attire reflect and speak of your hope of the heavenly attire? May your pilgrim journey through life be a witness for the King in all things.

[1]*Ancient and Modern Idolatry.* Clayton F. Derstine. Pg. 20   [2]*Ibid* Pg. 28.
[3]*Clothing, the Universal Language.* William Nicholson, 1988. Pg. 13.
[4]*Dress.* Mennonite Publishing House, 1935.
[5]*Christianity and Dress.* J. C. Wenger. Herald Press, 1944.
[6]*Set the Trumpet to Thy Mouth.* David Wilkerson. World Challenge, 1985. Pg. 144.
[7]*Clothing, the Universal Language.* William Nicholson, 1988. Pg. 61.
[8]*Ibid.*   [9]*Ibid*, Pg.18.   [10]*Ibid*, Pg. 64.   [11]*Ibid*, Pg. 51.
[12]*What About Setting Standards?* Rick Flanders. Vassem, Michigan.
[13]*Personal Appearance in Light of God's Word.* Lloyd Hartzler. Christian Light Publications.
[14]*What About Setting Standards?* Rick Flanders. Vassem, Michigan.

Questions for Discussion

1. Why do many ministers shrink from preaching a sermon on immodesty in dress?
2. What five earlier well-known evangelists and teachers denounced immodest dress?
3. a. How was Samuel's choice of Eliab, Jesse's oldest son, off the mark?
   b. Had he chosen Eliab because of his "better looks"?
4. Which gives the greater Christian freedom—the congregation with dress standards or the one without? Why?
5. How does the way one chooses to dress and to alter his or her natural appearance "make a statement" to others?
6. What do the decrees arrived at in Jerusalem (Acts 15) teach us about setting dress standards?

Questions submitted by
Paul Miller
Partridge, KS

You Can Find our Books at These Stores:

CALIFORNIA
Squaw Valley
  Sequoia Christian Books
  559/332-2385

GEORGIA
Glennville
  Vision Bookstore
  912/654-4086
Montezuma
  The Family Book Shop
  912/472-5166

ILLINOIS
Arthur
  Clearview Fabrics and Books
  217/543-9091
Ava
  Pineview Books
  584 Bollman Road

INDIANA
Goshen
  Country Christian Bookstore
  574/862-2691
Grabill
  Graber's Bookstore
  260/627-2882
LaGrange
  Pathway Bookstore
  2580 North 250 West
Middlebury
  Laura's Fabrics
  55140 County Road 43
Odon
  Dutch Pantry
  812/636-7922

  Schrock's Kountry Korner
  812/636-7842

Shipshewana
  E and S Sales
  260/768-4736
Wakarusa
  Maranatha Christian Bookstore
  219/862-4332

IOWA
Kalona
  Friendship Bookstore
  2357 540th Street SW

KANSAS
Hutchinson
  Gospel Book Store
  620/662-2875

KENTUCKY
Harrodsburg
  Family Bookstore
  859/865-4545
Stephensport
  Martin's Bookstore
  270/547-4206

LOUISIANA
Belle Chasse
  Good News Bookstore
  504/394-3087

MARYLAND
Grantsville
  Shady Grove Market and
    Fabrics
  301/895-5660
Landover
  Integrity Church Bookstore
  301/322-3311
Silver Spring
  Potomac Adventist Bookstore
  301/572-0700

**Our books may also be found on many
Choice Books bookracks**

Union Bridge
Home Ties
410/775-2511

MICHIGAN
Clare
Colonville Country Store
989/386-8686
Fremont
Helping Hand Home
231/924-0041
Sears
Hillview Books and Fabric
231/734-3394
Snover
Country View Store
989/635-3764

MISSOURI
Rutledge
Zimmerman's Store
660/883-5766
St. Louis
The Home School Sampler
314/835-0863
Seymour
Byler Supply & Country Store
417/935-4522
Versailles
Excelsior Bookstore
573/378-1925

NEW MEXICO
Farmington
Lamp and Light Publishers
505/632-3521

NEW YORK
Seneca Falls
Sauder's Store
315/568-2673

NORTH DAKOTA
Mylo
Lighthouse Bookstore
701/656-3331

OHIO
Berlin
Gospel Book Store
330/893-3847
Carbon Hill
Messiah Bible School
740/753-3571
Dalton
Little Country Store
330/828-2308
Fredricksburg
Faith-View Books
4941 Township Road 616
Hopewell
Four Winds Bookstore
740/454-7990
Mesopotamia
Eli Miller's Leather Shop
440/693-4448
Middlefield
Wayside Merchandise Books
and Gifts
15973 Newcomb Road
Millersburg
Country Furniture & Bookstore
330/893-4455
Plain City
Deeper Life Bookstore
614/873-1199
Sugarcreek
The Gospel Shop
330/852-4223

Troyer's Bargain Store
2101 County Road 70

**Our books may also be found on many
Choice Books bookracks**

PENNSYLVANIA

Belleville
Yoder's Gospel Book Store
717/483-6697
Chambersburg
Burkholder Fabrics
717/483-6697
Ephrata
Clay Book Store
717/733-7253

Conestoga Bookstore
717/354-0475

Home Messenger Library &
Bookstore
717/866-7605
Gordonville
Ridgeview Bookstore
717/768-7484
Greencastle
Country Dry Goods
717/593-9661
Guys Mills
Christian Learning Resource
814/789-4769
Leola
Conestoga Valley Books
Bindery
717/656-8824
Lewisburg
Crossroads Gift and Bookstore
570/522-0536
McVeytown
Penn Valley Christian Retreat
717/899-5000
Meadville
Gingerich Books and Notions
814/425-2835
Millersburg
Brookside Bookstore
717/692-4759

Narvon
Springville Woodworks
856/875-6916
Newville
Rocky View Bookstore
717/776-7987
Springboro
Chupp's Country Cupboard
814/587-3678
Stoystown
Kountry Pantry
814/629-1588

SOUTH CAROLINA
North Charleston
World Harvest Ministries
843/554-7960
Rembert
Anointed Word Christian
Bookstore
803/499-9119

TENNESSEE
Crossville
Troyer's Country Cupboard
931/277-5886
Sparta
Valley View Country Store
931/738-5465

TEXAS
Kemp
Heritage Market and Bakery
903/498-3366

VIRGINIA
Dayton
Books of Merit
540/879-5013

Mole Hill Books & More
540/867-5928

Rocky Cedars Enterprises
540/879-9714

**Our books may also be found on many
Choice Books bookracks**

Harrisonburg
  Christian Light Publications
  540/434-0768
Stuarts Draft
  The Cheese Shop
  540/337-4224

WEST VIRGINIA
Union
  Yoder's Select Books
  304/772-4153

WISCONSIN
Loyal
  Homesewn Garments
  715/255-8059

CANADA

BRITISH COLUMBIA
Burns Lake
  Wildwood Bibles and Books
  250/698-7451

ONTARIO
Brunner
  Country Cousins
  519/595-4277
Floradale
  Hillcrest Home Baking and
    Dry Goods
  519/669-1381
Millbank
  Lighthouse Books
  519/656-3058
Mount Forest
  Shady Lawn Books
  519/323-2830

**Our books may also be found on many
Choice Books bookracks**

Order Form

To order, send this completed order form to:
Vision Publishers, Inc.
P.O. Box 190
Harrisonburg, VA 22803
Fax: 540-437-1969
e-mail: visionpubl@ntelos.net

_____ _____
Name   Date

_____ _____
Mailing Address   Phone

_____
City   State   Zip

Don't Throw in the Towel   Qty. _____ x $6.99 each = _____

Where Has Integrity Gone?   Qty. _____ x $6.99 each = _____

What Shall the Redeemed Wear?   Qty. _____ x $7.99 each = _____

Price _____

Virginia residents add 4.5% sales tax _____

Grand Total _____

All Prices Include Shipping and Handling
All Payments in US Dollars

☐ Visa   ☐ MasterCard   ☐ Check #_____

CARD # __|__|__|__| __|__|__|__| __|__|__|__| __|__|__|__|

Exp. Date __|__|__|__|

For a complete listing of our books,
write for our catalog.
Bookstore inquiries welcome.